CONTENTS

Opposite: A view of the castle from the north-west.

HIGHLIGHTS

Stirling Castle's main buildings are arranged around the Inner Close, a large enclosure at the highest point. We recommend that you explore the whole castle and do not miss these highlights.

◀ THE ROYAL LODGINGS

The sumptuous, fashionable suite of apartments created by James V for himself and his aristocratic French bride, Mary of Guise. Interiors recreated in 2011 feature furniture, fittings, textiles and decoration of the time, but with the King's Lodgings left bare as they would have been following his untimely death in 1542 (p.16).

▲ THE GREAT HALL

Created by James IV in around 1503 as a spectacular setting for great state occasions. Recently restored to its former glory, this is the finest and largest medieval space in Scotland (p.14).

◀ THE CHAPEL ROYAL

The new chapel was built in 1594 by James VI for the baptism of his first son Prince Henry. This was the last great royal building to be erected in the castle, and one of the first Protestant kirks to be built in Scotland (p.12).

▲ VIEWS FROM THE LADIES' LOOKOUT

Here the royal family and their court looked down over elaborate terraced gardens and orchards to the king's hunting park beyond. You too can marvel at the dizzying vistas over the Vale of Menteith and the southern Highlands.

▲ THE FOREWORK

With this statement of splendour James IV announced himself as a great European ruler to all who approached his mighty castle (p.7).

◄ THE REGIMENTAL MUSEUM OF THE ARGYLL AND SUTHERLAND HIGHLANDERS

The Argyll and Sutherland Highlanders (Princess Louise's) were formed in 1881, when Stirling Castle became their depot. The regiment and its antecedents has served with distinction in virtually every conflict from the 1700s until the present day. The Museum is located in the King's Old Building and charts the regiment's long and distinguished history (p.29).

'IMAGE-MAKERS FOR THE KING' EXHIBITION ▶

This exhibition on the upper floor of the Palace explains how carving in wood and stone was cleverly used by James V to communicate powerful messages regarding his princely virtues and right to rule. At its heart are the original carved oak Stirling Heads which once adorned the Palace ceiling (p.25).

STIRLING CASTLE AT A GLANCE

The castle stands on a mighty volcanic crag sculpted by retreating ice sheets more than 10,000 years ago. Impregnable on three sides, its defences are focused on the more gently inclined approach from the south-east, where the town grew up. The castle's key strategic purpose was to control the crossing on the River Forth to the east.

Equalled only by Edinburgh Castle in its age and prestige, Stirling was in royal hands from at least 1110. It played a key role in the Wars of Independence (1296–1357) and over the centuries suffered 15 sieges. These included one of the last on British soil, when it was attacked by a force of Jacobites in January 1746. Its crowning glories are the buildings around the Inner Close, created by successive monarchs in the 1500s as an opulent setting for the Stewart court.

To Argyll's Lodging and Mar's Wark

Key

🏃 Tickets	👫 Toilet (male and female)
🎧 Audio guides	♿ Disabled toilet (male and female)
🏠 Information	🧍 Toilet (female)
🛍 Shop	🧍 Toilet (male)
🍴 Unicorn cafe	👶 Baby change

A ESPLANADE
Originally a narrow and rocky approach to the main gate, serving to emphasise the grandeur and elevation of the castle. The Esplanade was formed as a military parade ground in 1809.

B FRENCH SPUR
A defensive addition probably dating from the 1540s, when the widowed French queen Mary of Guise was in residence.

C OUTER DEFENCES
The outer defences and the dry ditch were added by the military engineer Theodore Dury during Queen Anne's reign (1708–14).

D GUARDROOM SQUARE
The ticket office and shop occupy a stables block built in the 1800s. Beyond, an inner gate leads to the Castle Exhibition.

E CASTLE EXHIBITION
An introduction to the castle, which explains how it was shaped by successive monarchs. It is housed in massive stone vaults known as casemates, built to house troops in the event of a siege.

F QUEEN ANNE GARDEN
Monarchs liked their gardens and there has been one here for at least 500 years, even though it stands outwith the main defences.

G FOREWORK
The impressive remains of the late-medieval frontage and entrance created by James IV, marking the line of the principal enclosure of the earlier castle.

H OUTER CLOSE
The lower and more public of the castle's principal courtyards.

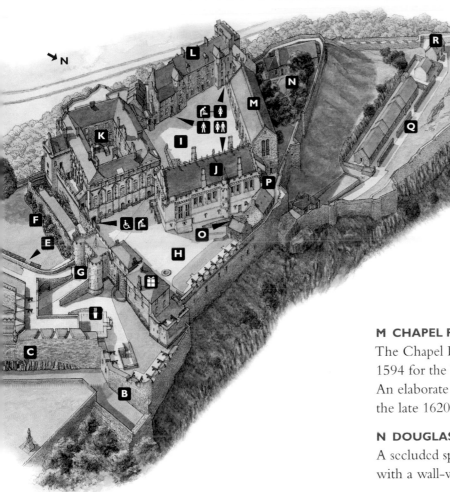

I INNER CLOSE

The summit of prestige, where in the 1500s successive Stewart kings created buildings to reflect the magnificence of their kingship.

J GREAT HALL

James IV's Great Hall, the largest ever built in Scotland, was completed in 1503 as a splendid venue for courtly celebrations and occasions of state.

K PALACE

A splendid royal residence commissioned by James V, who possibly never saw it completed. The palace's sumptuous royal apartments have been recreated in the style of the 1540s.

L KING'S OLD BUILDING

A fine suite of lodgings commissioned by James IV as his own residence, though it was much altered in later years for military use. It now houses the Regimental Museum of the Argyll and Sutherland Highlanders.

M CHAPEL ROYAL

The Chapel Royal was built by James VI in 1594 for the baptism of his first son, Henry. An elaborate frieze added for Charles I in the late 1620s still survives.

N DOUGLAS GARDENS

A secluded space at the rock's highest point, with a wall-walk overlooking the Forth valley.

O GREAT KITCHENS

Built during James IV's reign to prepare banquets for his Great Hall, the Great Kitchens have been reconstructed to show the cooks at work producing a feast.

P NORTH GATE

The oldest standing structure in the castle, dating back to the 1300s.

Q NETHER BAILEY

Originally a less secure area used for stores and crafts, but the defences here were strengthened in 1689. The area is now dominated by powder magazines built in 1810.

R TAPESTRY STUDIO

A temporary structure where visitors can watch weavers at work creating the tapestries to be hung in the Queen's Inner Hall.

S KING'S KNOT

The geometrically designed gardens date from the 1620s, but were created on the site of much earlier gardens.

THE OUTER DEFENCES

The approach from the town is now dominated by the business-like artillery defences created by Theodore Dury in the early 1700s. A renowned military engineer, Dury incorporated large parts of the French Spur built in the 1540s. These later defences mask the impressive towered frontage created by James IV.

THE FRENCH SPUR

Built with French money for Mary of Guise, the widow of James V, the Spur is still visible in the eastern frontal defences and dry ditch. Influenced by Italian military design, this is one of the best-preserved early stone-built artillery bastions in Scotland, with two tiers of guns covering the front and Stirling Bridge. The Spur was probably built by French troops fighting for the Scots, and a fleur-de-lis tablet can be seen on the eastern prow from the Ballengeich road immediately below the Spur. Part of the curved main prow is visible to the right of the main gate.

DURY'S OUTER DEFENCES

A major programme of defensive works was carried out between 1708 and 1714, and today's visitor is confronted by the resulting functional barrier. This could absorb cannon fire while also mounting an aggressive response. It has low-set, massively constructed walls, pepper-pot sentry boxes and a deep ditch, with a single entrance originally across a drawbridge. A flanking battery on the old Spur could fire along the front. Any attacker foolish enough to cross the ditch could be despatched by musket fire from defenders within two covered firing galleries known as caponiers, one of which now survives to the west of the entrance.

Top left: The Outer Defences.

Top centre: The gun platform of the French Spur.

Above left: Queen Anne's cipher above the inner gate in Guardroom Square.

Above right: A French fleur-de-lis carved on the exterior of the French Spur.

Guardroom Square sits immediately inside the defences. From here, an inner gate with the cipher of Queen Anne leads into the castle. Behind the defences were two sets of massive stone vaults, known as casemates, which could be used as barracks when under attack. Those overlooking the Queen Anne Garden now house the introductory Castle Exhibition.

THE FOREWORK –
'THE WHOLE OUTWARD BEAUTY OF THE PLACE'

Installed by James IV around 1500, the Forework now stands as a concealed inner entrance to the castle. But it was built as a highly visible façade, on a site that had long been the castle's main entrance. In the 1580s, it was described as 'the whole outward beauty of the place'.

The French Spur and Dury's Outworks masked a much earlier line of defence. Anyone approaching the castle in the early 1500s would have seen a very different frontage. The castle would have appeared far more elevated, with the visitor confronted by James IV's French-influenced frontispiece, immediately proclaiming his power and majesty.

It was originally five storeys high, but even in its much reduced state the Forework cannot fail to impress, integrating defensive and accommodation roles. Access to the main gate may originally have been by a timber bridge, rather than by the ramp in use today. The central triplet gatehouse was originally more than twice as tall, capped with crenellated wall-walks and tall conical roofs, and with a drum tower at each corner. Each of the three gates was provided with a portcullis, operated from the chambers above, and one of these still survives.

Overall, the gatehouse resembles the processional west door of a great church, and is even reminiscent of a Roman triumphal arch. The high curtain was bookended by an accommodation tower projecting at each end, flanked on each side a by a half-round tower (now demolished). The Elphinstone Tower on the east side was probably a self-contained lodging for the constable, with its own kitchen in the basement; the upper floors and chambers were removed in the later 1600s. Its twin to the west is the Prince's Tower, which still stands almost to full height with three floors and an attic.

Above left: The Forework as it is now.

Below: The Forework as it may have looked in James IV's time.

THE QUEEN ANNE GARDEN

Although the main gardens were always beneath the castle to the south-west, the area in front of the southern curtain may have been transformed into a garden as early as the 1400s, thereby creating an elegant outdoor space.

This tranquil garden may seem at odds with the warlike purpose of this vulnerable entrance side. A terraced walk from the Palace overlooking the west end of the garden was created against the Forework in the mid-1500s. Traces are still visible of balusters which enclosed the upper terrace. They were created in 1628–9, around the time when the gardens were transformed into a bowling green. The tree here is a beech and is more than 200 years old.

Right: The Queen Anne Garden, once used as a bowling green, overlooked by the Palace.

THE OUTER AND INNER CLOSES

The planning of the castle interior was dictated from early times by the constraints of the rocky topography, with some areas laboriously levelled for building on. The Outer Close reflects the service area for the late-medieval castle, with kitchens, the all-important main well, and chambers, all supporting the core royal life in the Inner Close.

The Forework entrance opens into the Outer Close, the lower of the two principal courtyards, now dominated by the Palace to the west and the gable of the Great Hall. On the south side of the close are the Main Guard House of the late 1700s and the Fort Major's House, built soon after.

Beyond these is the Elphinstone Tower, with a stair leading down into its two lower floors. At the far north end, beyond the Grand Battery of 1689, is the Master Gunner's House (1600s). Adjacent is the access to the Great Kitchens (see page 31).

The Inner Close marks the core of the 12th-century castle, whose defences and timber buildings have not survived. The only remnant might be the much-altered old chapel (not accessible) which stands behind the stair to the upper floor of the Palace. It was here in the Inner Close that James IV, James V and James VI created the sumptuous royal complex – the King's Old Building and Great Hall, the Palace and the Chapel Royal.

Above: The Inner Close, which gave access to the principal royal buildings of the 1500s.

JAMES V'S PALACE OF PRINCELIE VIRTUE

James V's wealth, learning and taste are reflected in the design of this new home for himself and his French queen, Mary of Guise. From the outset the Palace was designed to broadcast a coherent message – that James was a wise and virtuous ruler, whose reign would bring peace, prosperity and justice to the people of Scotland.

The Palace presents James V as he wished to be seen – as a king on a par with the greatest of European rulers. This is one of the earliest and most innovative pieces of Renaissance architecture in Britain, recently brought back to life by the recreation of the royal apartments. It is the most impressive building within the castle, with exuberant façades overlooking both the Inner and Outer Closes, and a third adjoining the western part of the Forework.

Building the Palace was a challenge. Archaeological investigations have shown that there were a number of pre-existing buildings here, on what had been the third close. These included the old chapel and a west range overlooking the royal park. This range may have provided accommodation for Margaret Tudor, wife of James IV. In addition there were possibly two or three other chamber blocks already here. Parts of these earlier buildings seem to have been retained and incorporated by the thrifty builders. The site sloped steeply to the south, which allowed them to build a series of service vaults, connected to a vaulted transe (passageway).

The builders overcame all sorts of difficulties to produce an extraordinary building, of pleasing proportions, with a fascinating stepped façade, alternating between large windows and life-size statues. But for all its modernity they cleverly incorporated a harking-back, by giving the Palace something of the bulk of an ancestral castle keep.

The statues were also revolutionary – their scale and subject matter had never been seen before in Scotland, reflecting a knowledge of Renaissance art and literature. The three decorated façades each presented an integrated tableau. Those on the east and north sides were intended to impress courtiers and ambassadors about to come into the royal presence. As they approached the entrance they would have passed beneath the statues on the north side, under the gaze of a full-size image of James. See pages 27–8 for a detailed discussion of the statues.

The builders cleverly produced an appearance of strict regularity, with the Palace planned around a central courtyard known as the Lion's Den, allegedly home to a lion bought in Flanders in 1537. The entrance was originally covered by a large porch probably resembling a Roman triumphal arch, which opened into the West Gallery. This passageway interconnected with the paired lodgings for the king and queen (see pages 16–24).

Opposite main picture: The Palace seen from the south-east, with the older Prince's Tower at the left and the Great Hall at the right.

Opposite bottom left: The statue of James V at the north-east corner of his Palace.

Opposite bottom centre: The statue of Abundance – one of five main figures on the north façade of the Palace.

Below: Part of the Palace's lavishly decorated south wall.

THE CHAPEL ROYAL

James VI had this magnificent chapel built in less than seven months in 1594, for the baptism of his first son, Prince Henry.

The construction of the Chapel Royal finally completed the regular arrangement of buildings around the Close begun 100 years earlier by James IV. At least one chapel would always have existed within the castle, an older one having stood at the south-west corner of the Inner Close. The building of the new Chapel Royal required the demolition of a chamber block, or possibly an earlier chapel, the outline of which can be seen laid out in the cobbles.

The large rectangular chapel is entered through an imposing doorway within a triumphal arch surround, with three paired windows on each side of the doorway. The doorway and windows were inspired by Classical Renaissance designs. According to a contemporary historian, the ceiling was decorated in gold and the walls were embellished with painted scenes and sculptures appropriate to a baptism.

The chapel fell out of use when the royal court moved to London in 1603, but was redecorated in 1628–9 by Valentine Jenkin in preparation for Charles I's coronation visit to Scotland in 1633. The best survival of this is the painted internal frieze. Its decorative frames are built around the Scottish royal regalia of crown, sword and sceptre, linked by flowers and fruit, with a *trompe l'oeil* window painted on the west gable.

Above: The exterior of the Chapel Royal, with the entrance as the focal point of an otherwise austere façade.

The building was later put over to military use, with partitions and floors inserted, while part of it seems to have been used as a garrison chapel into the late 1800s. A plan of 1870 shows the west part as a general store, with the rest divided into a chapel, a classroom and an armoury. By about 1900 it was only used for non-ecclesiastical functions. Much of the interior dates to the restoration of the 1930s and later, when the painted scheme was rediscovered.

Top: The Chapel Royal's expansive interior.

Above: The *trompe l'oeil* window painted on the west gable.

THE GREAT HALL

The grandest and best preserved element of James IV's ambitious building programme at Stirling, the Great Hall was to provide the spectacular setting for a century of state events. On completion in 1503 it became the largest secular space in the kingdom. On a daily basis, the Great Hall provided dining space for the humbler staff.

Above: The lion added to the roof of the Great Hall when it was restored in 1999. It echoes the lions surviving on the roof of the Palace.

Work began around 1500 to clear a site at the base of the eastern scarp of the Inner Close. An existing tower was demolished and its stones were reused. A vaulted service undercroft was created first, to provide level access from the close into the main entrance on the west side of the hall.

The hall was lit by high windows, except at the south end where a pair of projecting full-length bay windows gave prominence to the dais end, where the king and queen sat. Later on, this end was connected directly to the Palace by a bridge – a later version of this now provides the main entrance to the recreated Royal Lodgings of James V. The hall was heated by five fireplaces, including one for the monarch at the dais end. Four spiral stairs connect the various levels, giving access to a trumpeters' gallery, as well as to a minstrels' gallery above the screen near the entrance.

The original magnificent hammerbeam roof was removed at the end of the 1700s. It was replaced during the restoration of the hall, completed in 1999. The Great Hall is strongly medieval in character, with the usual features of a high-status building of this time, including niches for lost religious sculptures on the two long façades, a chequerboard corbel table, crow-stepped gables and crenellations, with English and Continental influences.

Now proceed over the bridge into the Palace, in which there are a number of staircases to negotiate. If you have difficulty with stairs, ask site staff about an accessible route into the Palace. Alternatively, visit the Access Gallery in the ground-floor transe.

This page: The Great Hall was commissioned by James IV. When completed in 1503 it was the largest and grandest building of its kind in Scotland.

THE PALACE: THE KING'S LODGINGS

The Royal Lodgings of James V and Mary of Guise have recently been recreated, based on years of expert research, to allow a full appreciation of how richly decorated and furnished these rooms would have been.

James V died in 1542, and may never have seen his Palace fully completed. Indeed, with the upheavals that followed, including attacks by Henry VIII's armies, it probably took a number of years to muster the resources to complete the work. The recreated King's Lodgings are therefore presented as only partly furnished and without a king, as would have been the case in the later 1540s.

Visitors enter the Palace over the bridge from the Great Hall and arrive in the King's Inner Hall, whose ceiling is gloriously decorated with replicas of the Stirling Heads. These were specially commissioned as part of the project to re-present the Palace interiors (see pages 18–19).

This was the presence chamber for audiences with the monarch. The decoration features *grisaille* paintwork, designed to mimic relief-carved stonework. The original fireplace with carved eagle capitals is dominated by the royal arms of Scotland painted above. The door to the Outer Hall is 16th-century, verified by dendrochronology (tree-ring dating), though it is not in its original position. This bare space may have been specially decked out for use during the coronation of the infant Mary Queen of Scots on 9 September 1543.

Next comes the King's Bedchamber, another
place where business was transacted, but in a
more convivial and confidential atmosphere.
The monarch was more likely to sleep in
one of the small closets off this chamber,
which would also have contained an altar
for personal devotions.

The Bedchamber's painted ceiling features
James V's crown alternating with his royal
cipher 'I5'. The central ceiling boss repeats
the royal arms, with other bosses recording
James's investiture in the great European
chivalric orders – the Golden Fleece
(Burgundy), St Michael (France), and the
Garter (England), along with the Scottish
heraldic thistle. Another splendid representation
of the royal arms is painted on the fireplace
overmantle, dominated by the unicorn, which
had been adopted by Scots kings as a symbol
of purity and strength. The fireplace front is
carved with more thistles.

Opposite: The King's Inner Hall.

Above left: The King's Bedchamber, left empty
in recognition of the king's death in 1542.

Left: A closer view of the fireplace in the King's
Bedchamber. The fireplaces may have been painted
in bright colours but, as part of the original fabric
of the Palace, they have been left unpainted.

THE STIRLING HEADS IN DETAIL

The Stirling Heads were not merely decorative. They embodied some of the key messages James V wanted to convey about himself and his court. The likely themes are represented in the exhibition of the original surviving Heads.

DYNASTY AND RIGHT TO RULE

The Stewart line of succession is represented by James IV and James I. James V's proximity to the English throne is represented by his mother, Margaret Tudor, and his overbearing uncle, Henry VIII. James himself is shown in his marriage coat, sewn with 50,000 pearls, flanked by both his French wives, with Mary of Guise depicted as a bride with a flower and flowing hair.

FRIENDS IN HIGH PLACES

Eager to move Scotland into the mainstream of European politics, James included his powerful allies in the scheme. These include Charles V, Holy Roman Emperor, the most powerful Catholic ruler in Europe. James's former father-in-law, King Francis I of France, is sure to have been carved, though the Head has not yet been found.

A KINGLY CODE

Among the figures depicted are fabled chivalric heroes known as Worthies, who embodied virtue and honour. Two are female, identified by their exotic headwear. An amazing discovery was spotted on number 20 – a harp tune carved into the border.

LEARNED LEADERS

James basked in the reflected glory of the greatest of the Roman emperors, while equating them with his own prowess as a political and military leader.

HERCULES THE HERO

James associated himself with Hercules as the ultimate moral man. This was made newly possible by the recent acceptance of Classical texts by the Roman Church.

MEET THE COURT

While some of the Heads underlined James's qualities and connections as a ruler, others give us glimpses of his glittering court. These are portraits in oak of nobles and courtiers dressed in the high fashions of Paris, Milan and London. Men are shown in velvet caps and slashed doublets, while the ladies' gowns are accurately detailed in the exuberant styles of the day. Some Heads probably portray French men and women of Mary's immediate circle. And we can be sure that the cosmopolitan connections did not end with the tailor. James, Mary and their courtiers were receptive to the latest ideas on politics, philosophy, art and religion of the Renaissance.

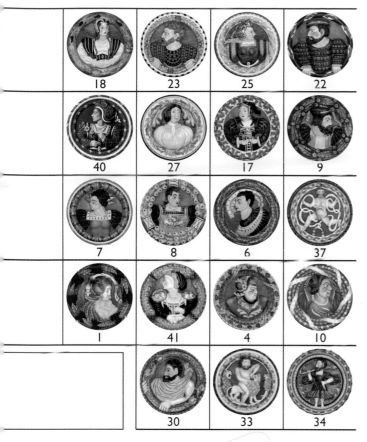

LOVE AND MARRIAGE

As well as proclaiming James's rule, the Palace also celebrated his marriage. Romantic and divine love is embodied in the dancing male children, known as *putti*, borrowed from the art of Renaissance Italy.

The Heads survived on the ceiling until it collapsed and had to be dismantled around 1777. They were then dispersed among a variety of individuals, and some were destroyed. It is thought that about ten of the Heads might have disappeared without record – and it is exciting to think that more may yet turn up.

Fortunately a record was made of the Heads soon after their dispersal, by Mrs Jane Graham, wife of the deputy governor of the castle. Her illustrations were published in a book of engravings entitled *Lacunar Strevelinense*, a copy of which is displayed in the exhibition upstairs. Most of the Heads were eventually collected into the Smith Art Gallery and Museum in Stirling, before they were returned to the castle.

PAGEANTRY AND COSTUME

The Heads also remind us of the importance of royal entertainments, including masques, plays and poetry. One Head depicts a lady in a masquing costume, while a poet is represented by the carving of a man with hand on heart in full poetic flow. This could even be Sir David Lindsay, an important advisor to the king as well as a leading playwright. Boisterous and irreverent fun is represented by the king's jester.

Numbering the Heads: The numbering system used to identify the Stirling Heads relates to their acquisition and was not used to inform the arrangement of the replica Heads on the ceiling.

The carvings numbered 15, 19, 21 and 35 survive only as fragments and are now recognised as likely to be from panelling. They are not shown here.

THE STIRLING HEADS AT A GLANCE

1	Male Worthy	23	Nobleman
2	Male Worthy	24	John, Duke of Albany
3	Male Worthy	25	Noblewoman
4	Male Worthy	26	Madeleine de Valois
5	Hercules	27	James IV
6	Roman emperor	28	Noblewoman
7	Julius Caesar	29	Woman in masquing costume
8	Emperor Titus	30	Hercules
9	James I	31	Roman emperor
10	Male Worthy	32	Roman emperor
11	Roman emperor	33	Hercules slays a lion
12	James V	34	Hercules with his club
13	Charles V	36	Jester
14	Poet	37	Putto
16	Noblewoman	38	Putto
17	Margaret Tudor	39	Henry VIII
18	Noblewoman	40	Mary of Guise
20	Female Worthy	41	Female Worthy
22	Nobleman		

THE QUEEN'S LODGINGS

This page: The richly furnished Queen's Bedchamber.

The next room is the Queen's Inner Hall, where she would have met honoured guests. The newly created painted ceiling includes portraits of James and Mary over the heraldic canopy above Mary's chair of estate, placed on a carpeted dais. It is possible that Mary originally had her own ceiling of carved heads, as more roundels existed than were required for just the King's Inner Hall. A visitor in 1731 describes 'two of these ceilings set of with ye well carved busts'.

The treasure here is the set of *Hunt of the Unicorn* tapestries (see pages 22–23). These are hung over decorated walls painted to look like hanging silk with a 'harebell' flower head design. Stools and benches have been provided for the dowager queen's attendants.

By contrast with the empty chambers of the deceased king, the Queen's Lodgings are fully furnished for a royal personage in residence. This was the home of Mary of Guise, James's French widow, who eventually assumed control of the nation as regent.

It was of course important for the Queen's Bedchamber to be adjacent to the King's, and so the queen's great state bed has been placed by the connecting door. The painted ceiling is of arabesque antique style, in gold leaf, centred on the heraldic arms of the de Guise family. The ceiling bosses display de Guise symbols: the Cross of Jerusalem and the alerion (three eagles shot with a single arrow). The royal and de Guise arms are combined on the cloth of estate, and Queen Mary's arms are repeated in the stained-glass window roundels.

The walls are hung with sumptuous brocaded cloth of gold, and Persian carpets are placed by the bed and on the table. A personal altar for Mary has been created with a French oak cupboard covered by an altar cloth and topped with a devotional triptych depicting the Virgin Mary. This would originally have been in her private closet rooms, now demolished.

Top left: A detail of the paintwork on the walls and ceiling of the Queen's Inner Hall.

Below: The triptych created for Mary of Guise's personal altar in the Queen's Bedchamber.

THE UNICORN TAPESTRIES

The tapestries depicting *The Hunt of the Unicorn* are a highlight of the recreated Palace interiors. Commissioned by Historic Scotland and some woven here in the castle, they are closely based on a set of 16th-century tapestries now in New York.

James and Mary owned many tapestries. An inventory of 1539 makes reference to two Unicorn sets – and this prompted the decision of which set to replicate for the re-created royal lodgings. The original tapestries would have been bought from workshops in the Low Countries, where a set of tapestries could cost almost as much as a new warship. As the royal court moved from one royal residence to another, the tapestries might be rolled up and transferred with their other possessions.

This set comprises seven tapestries which tell the story of the hunt of a unicorn in order to obtain its horn, believed to have magical powers of purification. The scenes are both decorative and instructive, being rich in Christian iconography, with the unicorn representing Christ, while the maiden symbolises the Virgin Mary. The climax comes with the killing and rebirth of the unicorn, representing the Passion and Resurrection. There were probably a number of different readings of the complex symbolism, including a more straightforward allegory of courtly love, where the unicorn (lover) is tethered and tamed by the maiden's love.

Each new tapestry takes between two and four years of painstaking work to produce. They are being woven by weavers from West Dean College in West Sussex, partly in the tapestry workshop in the Nether Bailey (see page 33). The set is due to be completed in 2013. The original tapestries are held in the Cloisters Museum of the Metropolitan Museum of Art in New York. The tapestry project has been part-funded by the Quinque Foundation of New York.

Top left: The Unicorn tapestries hanging in the Queen's Inner Hall.

Top right: 'The Unicorn Leaps out of the Stream' from the original series on which the replica tapestries have been based.

Above, clockwise from top left: Four of the new tapestries:
'The Start of the Hunt', 'The Unicorn is Found', 'The Unicorn in Captivity'
and 'The Unicorn is Killed and Brought to the Castle'.

THE OUTER HALLS AND WEST GALLERY

Beyond the queen's more intimate Bedchamber and Inner Hall, to which only privileged visitors would have had access, are more public spaces, where she might rub shoulders with lowlier subjects.

The Queen's Outer Hall was used both as a waiting room for those about to see Queen Mary, and for entertainments such as music and dancing. The queen would usually eat here too – informal meals were prepared in her own kitchen in the vaults below. Simple red decoration brightens the walls, based on contemporary examples surviving in Kinneil House, a noble residence in Bo'ness, between Stirling and Edinburgh. Note the distinctive French glazing pattern in the windows.

Leaving here, visitors pass through the West Gallery. This has purposefully been left bare as an archaeological space with evidence of later inserted floors and a stair. Approaching the exit it's possible to visit the King's Outer Hall, a waiting space equivalent to the Queen's Outer Hall. Courtiers cooling their heels here could enjoy the grotesque frieze and be impressed by the scale of the large royal arms painted on the overmantle. The mighty exterior oak door of the Palace is the original, remarkable for having survived hundreds of years of military occupation.

Above: The Parable Room at Kinneil House. When Stirling Palace was re-presented, these contemporary wall paintings helped determine the decorative scheme.

Left: The King's Outer Hall.

Opposite (top to bottom): The original Stirling Head showing the Jester; a drawing of the same Head, published in 1817; the replica Head commissioned by Historic Scotland from the sculptor John Donaldson; the final painted version of the replica.

THE STIRLING HEADS: IMAGE-MAKERS TO THE KING

The upper floor of the Palace is now occupied by the Stirling Heads Gallery. This is designed to explore court life at Stirling during the reign of James and Mary, based on the surviving evidence of carved decoration, chiefly the Stirling Heads and the exterior statues. Here we find some of the real evidence which has informed the recreated interiors on the floor below.

The stair up to the second floor was added around 1700 when new quarters were created for the castle governor. The entrance lobby features an astrological chart like the one drawn up for James V on his birthday in April 1512, where auspicious clues to his future fortune and fame would have been divined.

For James V, architecture was an important means of advertising carefully selected messages about his princely virtues, broadcast through the decorative arts. The building and its decoration proclaim the qualities, knowledge and virtues of James V as he wished to be seen – as a great European ruler.

This is embodied in the Stirling Heads. They were commissioned by James in about 1540 to adorn the ceiling of the King's Inner Hall, so that he could sit on his chair of estate with his credentials displayed on the ceiling above him. They were carved in the Renaissance style, which had arrived in France from northern Italy and was introduced to James's court by French craftsmen at the time of his second marriage, to Mary of Guise.

It is clear that a number of carvers executed the portraits and borders, some more competent than others. It may be that a small team of local craftsmen worked under the leadership of a French carver, Andrew Mansioun. James may never have seen his scheme completed before his death in 1542.

THE PRINCE'S TOWER AND PRINCE'S WALK

The Prince's Tower formed part of James IV's Forework, and was later incorporated into the south side of the Palace. This was traditionally the nursery of Scottish kings, including James VI.

The exit from the Stirling Heads exhibition is via a new stair inserted into the shell of the Prince's Tower and walk out onto the Prince's Walk. Faint graffiti has been found scratched into a window recess in a 16th-century script which reads: 'God made Man and [Wom]an God made Man, James 6'. This appears to be genuine.

Tree-ring dating of timbers from the tower have confirmed the early-16th-century date, while also indicating a refurbishment in 1593 in readiness for the birth of Prince Henry, son of the schoolboy scribe James VI, in the following year.

The Prince's Walk allows a close look at the grotesque and warlike sculptural tableau of the south façade of the Palace. These martial monsters are hurling missiles south against any potential invaders.

THE TRANSE

The base of the stair down from the Prince's Walk leads into the transe or passage under the south side of the Palace. This contains a number of service vaults, one of which was the queen's kitchen.

These are now decked out as exhibition spaces, dedicated to the occupations of the army of servants which supported royal life, featuring musicians, painters, tailors, carvers and even jesters. Another vault contains the Access Gallery, which allows remote access to displays in less easily reached parts of the castle.

Above: The Prince's Tower and Prince's Walk, with the south façade of the Palace at the right.

Right: Some of the many statues that adorn the external walls of the Palace. **1** Venus, goddess of love; **2** Saturn, god of time and agriculture; **3** The Devil; **4** One of many *putti*, or cherubs; **5** A watchful man-at-arms.

THE EXTERIOR SCULPTURES

The statues and sculpture lining the exterior walls of the Palace were intended to present James V as a powerful, just and learned monarch of the European Renaissance.

The exterior walls of the Palace are elaborately decorated with sculpture and statues. On top of the north and east walls, above the crenellated parapet, are statues of cherubs, some playing musical instruments; these contrast with the more warlike figures on the south wall. This feature would have helped unite the Palace with the roof lines of the other buildings. The parapet itself was drained by a run of splendid lion-headed waterspouts. Next down is a deep cornice inhabited by winged angels, providing divine protection to the anointed king and his family.

This is underlined by a spiralled ribbon wrapped around tree branches – one of several motifs that can also be seen on the Stirling Heads.

The large windows are inscribed above with the cipher 'I5' (James V). The statues were placed in recesses, sheltered by cusped arches with stops to either side of projecting humans or beasts. The figure of James at the north-east corner is crowned by the Scottish lion; he stands in an elegant pose borrowed from Classical sculpture, dressed in a fine doublet and hose, with one hand resting on the pommel of a dagger. All his portraits show him with a short beard, so his depiction here with a long beard might be intended to suggest a wise Old Testament prophet.

THE EXTERIOR SCULPTURES (CONTINUED)

James is supported by a square column decorated with a floral motif, which is repeated on a fireplace inside the Palace. He is supported by a column, which in turn stands on a corbel. From this projects a sculpted noblewoman in contemporary dress – a figure who may represent Fame. At the very base is a much eroded lion couchant, the heraldic symbol of the English king – in this case perhaps crushed by the Scots king!

James looks down on the visitor, placing himself beside the Classical gods Saturn and Venus. The message was there to be understood by the learned visitor – James was the legitimate leader stemming from an ancient dynasty, whose virtuous rule would produce a new golden age (Saturn) of peace (Venus) and plenty. Next to James stands Ganymede, the cup-bearer to the gods. In this case, he symbolises the eternal youth to be provided by James's new golden age. The figure of Abundance above the door showers visitors with the fruits of his just reign.

Overall the artistic influences are derived from French palaces connected to the de Guise family, though the statues on columns were inspired by ancient Rome. James himself had spent much of 1536 in France with his mason Moses Martin, who was no doubt preparing ideas for the embellishment of the Scottish royal residences for the arrival of the king and queen.

DID YOU KNOW. . .

James V was the seventh monarch of the Stewart royal dynasty. The family came from France via England, and from the 1100s occupied the hereditary title of 'steward' to the king. After Robert II claimed the throne in 1371, the crown passed in an unbroken line from father to son. On his deathbed in 1542, James V predicted 'it'll gang wi' a lass' ('it will end with a girl'). He is thought to have been referring to his daughter and successor, Mary Queen of Scots. But how wrong he was: her son James VI acceded to the thrones of both Scotland and England, adopting the French spelling 'Stuart'. The dynasty continued until 1714, when Queen Anne, its 14th monarch, died without living issue.

Above left: James V dominates the north-east corner of the Palace.

THE KING'S OLD BUILDING

Left: The King's Old Building as it may have looked around 1500, when it housed the royal apartments of James IV.

Inset: The King's Old Building today.

At the core of the range known as the King's Old Building are the royal lodgings of James IV. These date back to 1496, and command magnificent views to the west across Flanders Moss and towards Loch Lomond.

James IV's royal lodgings were L-shaped in plan, incorporating walls of an older building at the south end of this site. The main apartments were on the first floor, approached by a spiral stair in an entrance tower capped by an octagonal superstructure.

The first-floor rooms originally rose to the full height of the building, opening into the roof, with large windows onto the Inner Close. The stair opened into the king's hall, beyond which was his chamber, with lesser chambers in the cross range at the north end. The room to the south of the hall was probably a kitchen, with timber galleries in front looking onto the close. This suite originated as James IV's bachelor lodgings. After he married Margaret Tudor in

1503, lodgings for the queen were probably formed in the old west range, later incorporated into the Palace. The old chapel was located between the two lodgings.

From the later 1600s onwards, the King's Old Building was substantially altered for military use. By the 1800s it provided married quarters and a sergeants' mess. It now houses the regimental museum of the Argyll and Sutherland Highlanders. Many regiments were stationed in the castle up until 1881, when it became permanent depot of the newly amalgamated Princess Louise's Argyll and Sutherland Highlanders. All recruits received basic training here, up to 150 at a time, until the Argylls finally marched out in 1964. In 2006, the regiment was transformed into the 5th Battalion, The Royal Regiment of Scotland. Their museum houses fascinating displays telling the story of the regiment from the Peninsular War (1807–14) up until recent conflicts, with battle dioramas, weapons, regalia and spectacular regimental silver.

THE DOUGLAS GARDENS AND WALL-WALKS

As the highest part of the castle rock, the site of the Douglas Gardens is likely to have been the focus of the early earthwork castle. Nothing of this survives apart from the original defensive line fossilised in the north curtain wall. There have been gardens here since the 1500s.

By the time the Chapel Royal was built here in 1594, any vestiges of the older earthworks had been levelled to create the Douglas Gardens. The name is derived from the tradition that this is where the body of the 8th Earl of Douglas was dumped after he was murdered by James II in 1452.

Above: The National Wallace Monument, visible from the wall-walk.

Top right: The Douglas Gardens, with the King's Old Building in the background.

Fine views can be had from the 18th-century wall-walk. To the east, the River Forth snakes around the bell-tower of Cambuskenneth Abbey. Established by David I around 1140, Cambuskenneth was later the burial place of James III and his wife Margaret of Denmark. To the north is Stirling Bridge, built in stone in the 1400s close to the site of the older timber bridge, where the Scots defeated the English in 1297 (see page 40). Beyond this are the wooded slopes of Abbey Craig, where the army led by Andrew Murray and William Wallace formed up for battle, inflicting a devastating defeat on Edward I's forces. This is powerfully commemorated by the National Wallace Monument, built on the peak in the 1860s in honour of Scotland's freedom fighter. It is framed behind by the Ochill Hills.

THE GREAT KITCHENS AND NORTH GATE

When James IV built his Great Hall he also had Great Kitchens built to cater for his magnificent feasts, and to provide food for the household on a daily basis. These were conveniently sited at the back, against the east curtain wall of the Outer Close, far enough away from the hall to avoid any fire hazard.

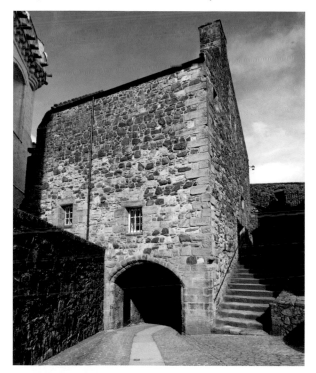

The kitchens were infilled and the area massively built up in 1689 to create the Grand Battery, although the kitchens were rediscovered and excavated in 1921. The kitchens, including a bakehouse and cold storage, have now been reconstructed with displays showing preparations for a feast. We cannot be sure how the food reached the hall from the serving hatches. It was either carried across the close (now greatly raised up) or else along a corridor which linked to the first floor of the North Gate.

The North Gate is probably the oldest standing building in the castle, parts of which date to 1381. It was extended and heightened on a number of occasions, but the most extensive works were in 1511–12, when an everyday kitchen to serve the Great Hall was constructed on the first floor. This gate provided access to and from a postern gate (back door) and the Nether Bailey.

Left: The North Gate, the oldest surviving building in the castle.

Below: Preparing a meal in the re-created Great Kitchens.

This page: The Nether Bailey seen from above. The row of stone buildings are powder magazines, built a safe distance from the rest of the castle around 1810.

THE NETHER BAILEY

The Nether Bailey is a large, irregular lower enclosure to the north of the main part of the castle. It is likely to have been enclosed as part of the early earthwork castle.

The Nether Bailey probably always functioned as a service area for the castle, with stables, stores and workshops, as well as the royal dog kennels. The steepness of the rock here makes it unlikely that there was ever a main entrance to the castle at this point, although the remains of two small postern gates can be seen, one each to the east and west. These provided concealed access at times of siege. They were probably blocked when the defences were strengthened in 1689.

Within the Nether Bailey are a Guard House and four powder magazines, built around 1810. Three of the magazines are surrounded by a high wall and covered by parabolic vaults in case of explosion. These three were interconnected in 1908 and converted for use as transit stores. There was also a miniature rifle range here.

The Nether Bailey also houses the tapestry studio, where weavers are completing the Unicorn tapestry series displayed in the Queen's Inner Hall in the Palace.

THE TAPESTRY STUDIO

The Unicorn tapestries hanging in the Queen's Inner Hall are being created by weavers from West Dean College, Chichester. Three of the tapestries have been produced at West Dean; the other four in the purpose-built temporary studio here in Stirling. Until the completion of the project in 2013, visitors to the castle can watch the weavers at work, with daily talks in the studio at 1pm.

The designs for the tapestries are closely based on a set held at the Cloisters Museum in New York. The weavers were allowed special access to the original tapestries, studying them closely to analyse techniques, patterns and colours.

However, there are key differences in approach and materials. Unlike the originals, the new tapestries have been woven from the front rather than the back – allowing both the weavers and the public to see the finished designs taking shape. Modern chemical dyes have been used in place of traditional ones, and mercerised cotton thread is used instead of more perishable silk. The new tapestries also omit the cipher 'AE' which appears in all the originals.

In addition, the weavers have created completely new sections to replace damaged and missing portions of the original tapestries. Nowhere has this been a greater challenge than with 'The Mystic Hunt of the Unicorn', of which only two fragments survive.

DID YOU KNOW...

In heraldry, the unicorn is the supporter of the royal arms of Scotland. This mythical creature was believed to have special powers of protection and purification. It was adopted as a heraldic emblem around the early 1400s and is depicted to this day in Scottish representations of royalty. It is likely that this magical beast featured on a set of tapestries owned by James V, and this series has been newly produced and displayed in the Palace.

THE RECREATIONAL LANDSCAPE

The surrounding landscape was dedicated to supporting royal recreation and court life in the castle. Generations of Scottish royalty could gaze down on the south-western slopes and plain to view their park, gardens, and tournament grounds. This provided essential amenities for which there was no space within the castle.

An enclosed hunting ground for the castle, known as the Royal Park, existed from the early 1100s on the site where the golf course now stands. Around 1500, James IV had its embanked boundaries improved, and restocked it with animals. White cattle grazed in the park, which was not just a place for hunting deer and wild boar. Horses were pastured on the plain, as well as oxen to pull the royal gun train, while hay for animal feed and cereals for the table were produced in neighbouring fields.

Part of the baptismal celebrations for the infant Prince James (later James VI) were played out in the Valley, the dip between the Esplanade and Holy Rude Kirkyard, while ground to the south-east was known as the Play Yard, possibly used for outdoor entertainments. There were royal tennis courts in the town. Judicial executions took place on the 'heading hill' close by. The area around the castle was generally maintained free of tree cover to allow clear sight-lines on any attackers, including a clear line down as far as Stirling Bridge. The stables and royal laundry were also located below and to the west, near where the fire station stands today, not just for reasons of space but also because of the limited water supply in the castle.

Jousting was important for the king as a means of demonstrating both his warlike prowess and his chivalric qualities as defender of the faith. The tournament yard had stood to the south of the castle, but in 1507 it was moved to the west by James IV, to be at the heart of the recreational landscape. It is recorded that James V was a regular and enthusiastic participant in mounted, chivalrous combat. The archery practice butts also stood here.

Above: The formal pleasure grounds known as the King's Knot, probably laid out in the 1620s.

The King's Knot is the last vestige of extensive gardens which date back to at least the mid-1400s. James IV was a keen gardener, acquiring many seeds, plants and trees. He probably created terraced gardens on the slopes between the Knot and Stirling's churchyard, now densely overgrown. There was a loch with ornamental swans and herons. Gardens with vegetable plots, fish ponds and orchards existed on the Knot site, and over a thousand young trees were planted in 1497 to create avenues and arbours. New varieties were highly prized, and when Mary of Guise arrived for her wedding in 1538 she brought cuttings from plum and pear trees. Vestiges of this orchard still existed in the early 1700s.

The King's Knot formal pleasure grounds were probably made in 1627–9 by master gardener William Watts, in anticipation of a homecoming by Charles I. The geometric lines would have been defined with low box-hedging and planting within raised beds. The earthworks of the Knot might have disappeared altogether had it not been for a visit in 1842 by Queen Victoria, who bemoaned the poor condition of the gardens. By 1866 the earthworks had been repaired to the state in which they survive today.

Top right: A jousting display at Linlithgow Palace. Jousting tournaments were a favourite pastime of James IV and James V.

Right: The miniature 'enchanted fortress' temporarily erected in the Valley in 1566 to celebrate James VI's baptism. The Esplanade now covers the site once occupied by the Valley.

THE HISTORY OF STIRLING CASTLE

The great royal fortress of Stirling was both symbolically and strategically important for centuries. It commanded the countryside for miles around, looking south and east along the Forth valley towards Edinburgh, while also looking out to the wild Highlands and the Gaelic west.

It has been described as 'a huge brooch clasping the Highlands and Lowlands together', overshadowing Stirling Bridge and thereby controlling movement across the Forth. No wonder successive sovereigns made such a great investment in developing the castle as a projection of their lordship. Stirling's national importance is seen in the key role it played in the Wars of Independence, resulting in terrible damage. But the castle was rebuilt and rebuilt again – consequently only the later buildings survive above ground. These remarkable buildings were created as the backdrop for the glittering courts of James IV, James V, Mary Queen of Scots and James VI – Renaissance monarchs who put Scotland on the European map.

CASTLE ROCK

The rock on which Stirling Castle stands started life when a volcano erupted around 350 million years ago. The solidified lava was slowly buried under sandstone sediments and ice, and when the ice melted the rock was sculpted by retreating glaciers.

The result was an almost impregnable stronghold. The faces to north and west are nearly vertical, while the formation of rock to south and east has predetermined the siting of buildings and defensive circuits.

For centuries, the Ochils and Touch Hills, east and west of Stirling, forced anyone travelling between northern and southern Scotland to pass close to Stirling. Here they also encountered important roads to east and west. Stirling Castle was therefore at a crossroads; it also controlled the most convenient crossing of the River Forth at Stirling Bridge, and Stirling's small harbour. This combination of natural defences and strategic location made Stirling an irresistible site for a stronghold.

The earliest fortification probably dates back more than 3,000 years, although hardly any evidence survives. It is certainly likely that in the centuries just before the Roman invasion (around AD 80) the Maeatae or Votadini tribe established a hillfort on the rock. A smaller fort has been found on the Gowan Hill to the north, and the two forts may have co-existed.

Tradition states that Agricola, leader of the Roman army during the conquest of Scotland, fortified Stirling castle rock. The English chronicler William of Worcester, writing in the 1400s, identified Stirling as the home of King Arthur's Knights of the Round Table, and this myth was repeated by later writers.

These stories are at best dubious, but they do chart early assertions of antiquity associated with the castle, as a place which lent itself to mythmaking, strengthening the ancestral claims of later kings.

Below: The castle rock (centre), with the Abbey Craig at the left, topped by the National Wallace Monument.

A MEDIEVAL CASTLE

Above: William I, known as 'The Lion', was an early occupant of Stirling Castle, who enjoyed hunting in the surrounding forest.

It is only from the late 11th century that Stirling Castle begins to emerge as a historical reality. Not long after, it was considered suitable for royal occupation.

The earliest known reference to Stirling is in the *Life of St Monenna*, written in the late 11th century by a scholar called Conchubranus. Evidence of a royal role for Stirling comes not long afterwards, around 1110. At this time, King Alexander I made arrangements for the financial support of a chapel already existing in the castle, newly dedicated to St Michael. This is probably on the site of the chapel recently discovered between the King's Old Building and the Palace.

As a royal castle, Stirling had to provide residential accommodation for the king and his court, but it also had to house his administrative officers. Around 1140, David I founded Cambuskenneth Abbey nearby, partly to meet his secretarial and spiritual needs. A symbol of the king's power, this mighty castle was the focus of rich royal estates in the area, which provided much of the enormous quantity of food consumed when the household was in residence.

High-status buildings of royal government and accommodation were probably based on the three terraces of the summit, divided into an upper and lower courtyard, much as they are today. The summit would have been enclosed by ramparts of earth, rock and turf, some of which were already old by the early 1100s. The highest point is now the Douglas Gardens, and this could have been the site of the king's hall. All the buildings were probably of timber, except the chapel, which would have been of stone.

William I (1165–1214) had part of the royal forest embanked to maintain good stocks for the hunt. Stirling was surrendered to Henry II of England in 1174, as part of the price paid for William's release from captivity, although the castle was never occupied by the English at this time.

TIMELINE

AROUND AD 80

AGRICOLA
is said to have established a stronghold on the castle rock during the Roman invasion of Scotland.

AROUND 1110

ALEXANDER I
funds maintenance of a chapel within the castle – the first record of royal activity at Stirling.

THE WARS OF INDEPENDENCE

Inevitably, Stirling's great symbolic and strategic importance dictated a central role for the castle in the resistance to English overlordship in the late 1200s and early 1300s.

Scotland had enjoyed a lengthy peace with England until the untimely death of Alexander III in 1286. This caused a breakdown in royal succession and put the two countries on a collision path. The death of Alexander's granddaughter and heir, Margaret, the Maid of Norway, in 1290, left no clear heir. Edward I of England was invited to adjudicate between rival claimants, and he briefly stayed in Stirling in 1291 during this process. Ultimately Edward favoured John Balliol, Lord of Galloway, who was made king the following year.

But when King John's nobles negotiated a treaty with France against England in 1295, this unleashed Edward I's fury, resulting in decades of intermittent warfare known as the Wars of Independence. Edward swept north in 1296 – earning the nickname 'Hammer of the Scots' – and stripped Balliol of his crown. Stirling Castle was captured, and it was the Scots' determination to regain this great prize which led to their victory at the Battle of Stirling Bridge in 1297 (see panel). This triumph was short-lived, however. The following year, the Scots were routed at the Battle of Falkirk.

Edward I died in 1307 while preparing to invade Scotland once more. On his deathbed, he ordered that his bones be carried into battle against the Scots. The death of the feared king, coupled with the inspired leadership of Robert I (the Bruce), led to rapid improvements in Scottish fortunes. By 1313, only Stirling and three other castles remained in English control. King Robert's younger brother Edward Bruce laid siege to Stirling, but reached an understanding with the garrison captain, Sir Philip Moubray, that the castle would be surrendered to the Scots if it had not been relieved by the English by Midsummer's Day 1314. It was the determination of Edward I's son and successor Edward II to retain Stirling which led to the Battle of Bannockburn, undoubtedly the most important victory in Scottish military history.

THE BATTLE OF STIRLING BRIDGE

In September 1297 the aged Earl of Surrey led a large English force to camp beneath the castle, then in English hands. They found a Scottish army, led by William Wallace and Andrew Murray, drawn up in a strong defensive position on the Abbey Craig, on the far side of the river. When the English knights eventually crossed the narrow timber bridge, the Scots sprang a two-pronged trap, and their spearmen massacred the cavalry caught on the bridge. Those who had already crossed were caught in a loop of the River Forth. To cut his losses, Surrey ordered the bridge destroyed, sealing the fate of his troops on the north bank. This was a humiliating defeat for the English, but ironically it prompted them to unite behind their king and provide sufficient resources to crush the rebels in the north. When the two armies next met, at Falkirk in 1298, the Scots were defeated.

Opposite: The closing stages of the siege of Stirling Castle in 1304. At this time, Stirling was the last major stronghold left in Scottish hands and it withstood the onslaught of Edward I for three months. Ultimately, Edward sent for his fearsome 'war wolf' siege engine and would not accept surrender until it had been used.

1296

1297

EDWARD I
of England invades Scotland in the first wave of what will be 60 years of bitter cross-border warfare.

WILLIAM WALLACE
and Sir Andrew Murray lead Scottish forces to victory at the Battle of Stirling Bridge.

THE BATTLE OF BANNOCKBURN

The greatest battle in Scottish history was fought in the boggy plain two miles south of Stirling Castle in June 1314.

Edward II took up the challenge laid down by Edward Bruce of relieving the beleaguered English garrison at Stirling. He crossed the border with a 17,000-strong army, moving in haste to meet the deadline. King Robert's army of 8,000 Scots barred their way. On 23 June, the English vanguard made a hasty attack, during which King Robert was engaged by Sir Henry de Bohun. The sight of their king splitting open the young knight's skull inspired the Scots to repulse the charge.

King Robert knew that Bannockburn was risky. Until now he had favoured guerrilla tactics, avoiding pitched battles because of the English superiority of numbers. But when he learned of his enemy's low morale he decided to stand and fight. On Midsummer's Day, 24 June, the English advanced from weak positions, and after a bitter encounter their cavalry was crushed by the Scottish schiltrons (formations of spear-wielding infantry).

Bruce had his small cavalry force overrun the English archers, and then unleashed his brigade of Highlanders and Islesmen, pushing the English into the boggy ground. Many were caught between the Bannock Burn and the River Forth and were massacred, leaving the burn choked with English dead.

Edward II's court poet was captured and forced to compose victory verses for the Scots. A fabulous booty was looted from the baggage train, which was said to stretch all the way back to Edinburgh, and rich sums were earned from ransoming captured knights. This greatest of victories gave strategic control of Scotland back to King Robert. It also resulted in an exchange of prisoners, which was a personal victory for Bruce. His wife Queen Elizabeth, together with his daughter Marjorie, and his great political ally Bishop William Wishart had all been imprisoned in England since 1306. There was a joyous return made possible by a trade of English nobles.

Top: A reconstruction illustration of the Battle of Bannockburn, 24 June 1314.

STIRLING CASTLE UNDER SIEGE

'…And stood against him,
Proud Edward's army,
And sent him homeward
To think again.'

Roy Williamson, 'The Flower of Scotland',
1967 © The Corries (Music) Ltd

Between 1296 and 1342, Stirling Castle spent more time occupied by the English than the Scots. This wrought havoc on the castle buildings.

Some sieges were quick, while others lasted months, and life in the castle would have deteriorated rapidly. Food supplies were limited, and the castle always suffered from a poor water supply. However, supplies may have been brought in through the northern posterns, either smuggled in or else by chivalrous agreement.

By this time, the curtain walls, the gatehouse and some other buildings were built of stone, although many of the accommodation and service buildings would still have been of timber, with wattle-and-daub walls and turf roofs. These would all have taken a terrible pounding. The accounts of 1336–7 record extensive repairs and rebuilding. Guns were now being used, coupled with a bone-breaking array of siege engines, deployed to devastating effect.

1296	Captured by Edward I.
1297	Retaken by Scots following victory at the Battle of Stirling Bridge.
1298	Recaptured by the English after defeat of the Scots at Falkirk.
1299	Besieged again and surrendered to the Scots by the Constable John Samson. The starving English released by the Scots following chivalrous conventions of war.
1304	Now the only significant stronghold left in Scots control, besieged by Edward I for three months. For this major campaign, a pontoon bridge is constructed in King's Lynn in Norfolk and floated up the east coast, enabling Edward's forces to cross the River Forth downstream from Stirling. Edward refuses to accept surrender until he has tried out the 'war wolf' on the castle walls. This is a large, powerful trebuchet (siege catapult) which took 445 workmen to build. The Scots defenders, commanded by Sir William Oliphant (commemorated in a plaque on the King's Old Building), are marched out and ritually humiliated as traitors, but not executed.
1313	Edward Bruce commences siege.
1314	Retaken by the Scots after Edward II is defeated at Bannockburn.
1336	Retaken by the English.
1342	Finally back in Scottish control after a siege lasting six months.

1314

EDWARD II
arrives in Scotland with a 17,000-strong army, aiming to relieve the English garrison holding Stirling Castle on his behalf.

1314

KING ROBERT I (THE BRUCE)
confronts Edward's army at Bannockburn and inflicts a strategic victory.

AFTER BANNOCKBURN

The humiliating disaster of Bannockburn dealt a severe blow to Edward II's ambitions, but this was not to be a permanent reversal. With the death of King Robert in 1329, a new struggle broke out for control of the kingdom.

Immediately after the Battle of Bannockburn, Edward II tried to take refuge in Stirling Castle, but Sir Philip Moubray stuck to his bargain and handed it back to the victorious Scots. This resulted in further damage to the castle: King Robert had learned that the best policy was to render a captured castle indefensible, rather than risk letting it fall back into enemy hands.

Following the abdication of Edward II in 1327, King Robert invaded northern England. This led to the Treaty of Edinburgh in 1328, a final acknowledgement of Scotland's territorial integrity. But sadly the old king did not live long to enjoy the peace. He died the following year, and was succeeded by his five-year-old son David II.

Disaffected Scots nobles took advantage of the instability caused by David's minority. They encouraged Edward Balliol – exiled son of the late King John, regarded by many as the rightful king – to invade in 1332. His campaign stalled in 1334 but was enthusiastically supported by Edward III, who stepped into his grandfather's boots, and sent the young David II into exile in France for seven years. Stirling was captured in 1336 and many repairs carried out to improve both the defences and the accommodation of the castle. It was not until 1342 that it was retaken by the Scots.

THE OLD CHAPEL BURIALS

Recent archaeological investigations threw up an important and exciting discovery – a lost royal chapel. But a bigger surprise came when skeletons were found buried beneath its floor. Two of these were especially exciting – a man and a woman who had both suffered violent deaths in battle in the 1300s.

Excavations were begun under a building dating back to the 1600s, known as the Governor's Kitchen. We now understand that this was on the site of a large chapel, the east end of which was built over when the Palace was constructed around 1540. Nine graves were found underneath the floor of the nave at the west end of the chapel. Two of those interred were a baby and an infant, while the others had lived to about 14 to 40 years old. Their bones were radiocarbon dated, revealing that they were buried from the 1200s to the early 1400s.

Two of the dead have proved to be of great interest: a man and a woman who probably died in the 1300s. Forensic analysis showed the man's skull had a healed injury from a sword or axe cut, which had probably smashed through his helmet into the top of his head.

Right: The grand seal of Edward Balliol, son of King John, regarded by many as the rightful heir to the Scottish throne.

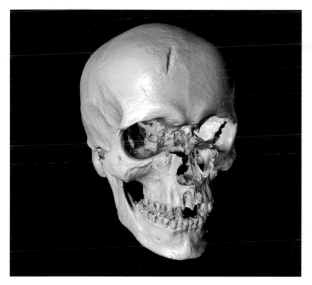

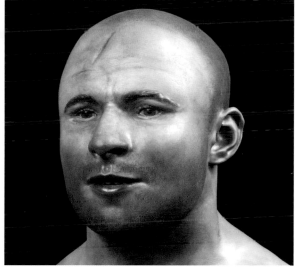

He also had a barbed arrowhead lodged in his chest, which may have been the cause of death. Other evidence showed he had an extremely well-muscled upper body, was bow-legged from horse riding, and was in his mid-20s when he died, after a short and violent life. Together the evidence suggests he was a knight, and further analyses have indicated that he probably grew up in the south of England.

Analysis of the woman's skeleton revealed she was also robustly built, but slightly older than the knight. She too had suffered a violent death, killed by a double blow to her skull from a mace.

Burials in castle chapels are very unusual, and they would certainly not have included any royal burials. But burial in this prestigious location would indicate that the deceased were of high status, probably buried here out of necessity, perhaps when the castle was cut off in times of siege. Had they been caught in skirmishes beyond the walls, or were they defenders who suffered at the hands of Scots winning back their prized castle of Stirling? Most of the other burials have suffered blunt weapon trauma indicating death in combat, although the circumstances are far from clear.

Above: A 3D scan of the skull belonging to a man whose remains were found buried under the old royal chapel. He had survived the head wound but was killed by a later injury.

Above: A model shows how the man's features may have looked. He had a very muscular upper body and would have had a prominent scar on his forehead.

1334

EDWARD III
revives his grandfather's claim on Scotland and sends David II into exile.

1342

STIRLING CASTLE
is finally retaken by the Scots, following a six-month siege.

THE CASTLE IN THE LATER MIDDLE AGES

After the Wars of Independence, Stirling Castle continued to develop at the heart of the nation's affairs, and its role as a royal residence grew in importance.

In 1371, Robert the Steward came to the throne as Robert II, establishing Scotland's greatest dynasty, the royal Stewarts. Siege damage from earlier in the 1300s was repaired and the new North Gate was constructed in 1381. The castle's role as a royal nursery was formalised, and Stirling certainly offered appropriate security and iconic status.

After James I returned from captivity in England in 1424, he granted the castle to his queen, Joan Beaufort, as part of her marriage settlement. She held it as her own property, along with the income required to support it from the local estates known as the Lordship of Stirling. This practice was repeated by many of James's successors.

More gravely, Stirling was where James I settled scores against those he felt had done too little to obtain his release. The main culprit was his uncle, Robert, Duke of Albany, but as he had died in the castle in 1420, James's wrath was redirected against his son, Murdoch, who had succeeded his father as governor of the realm. The sentence of death was ratified by Parliament at Stirling in May 1425. Murdoch, his two sons, and the 80-year-old Earl of Lennox were beheaded on the 'heading hill' close to the castle. This ruthless act brought James their considerable forfeited wealth. However, this and other actions made him many enemies and he was assassinated in Perth in 1437.

Little building is recorded during the reign of James II (1437–60), but Stirling was still a much favoured royal residence. James had certainly inherited a ruthless streak from his father, which he directed against his leading noble family, the grand and successful Douglases. This confrontation came to a head in Stirling in February 1452 when the fiery young king lost his temper and stabbed William, 8th Earl of Douglas, to death. The traditional site for this murder is in the King's Old Building, which in fact had not been built by then.

IAMES THE FIRST IN MARIAGE DIDGET
NANS DOCHTER TO YE ERLI OF SOMERSET
ANE INGLIS LORD OF HONOVR AND RENOVN
THIS IAMES THE FIRST SCHORT QVHILE
POSSEST THE CROVN

Left: A page from the *Forman Armorial*, produced around 1562, shows King James I and his wife Joan Beaufort. She was the first in a line of queen consorts to receive Stirling Castle as a marriage gift.

James III (1460–88) considered Stirling to be 'his most pleasant residence', and seems to have commissioned more building work than his father. Accounts show work on an unidentified 'white tower' in 1463, and repairs to the castle walls and the Chapel of St Michael around 1467. He was also building up the royal gun train, and guns were cast within the castle in 1475. James III may even have started work in laying out the Great Hall.

He was on poor terms with his wife, Margaret of Denmark, who spent the last three years of her life in the castle, largely apart from her husband. She was accompanied by her son, the future James IV, and he remained in residence after his mother's death in 1486. Two years later, he was persuaded to leave the castle to join with disaffected nobles who had risen against his father the king. Prince James's presence helped ensure the defeat and subsequent assassination of James III at Sauchieburn, close to Bannockburn. In succeeding to the throne, James IV made confession of his role in the regicide in the royal chapel in Stirling Castle.

Above: Two painted panels from an altar-piece show James III (left, with his son, the future James IV, and St Andrew) and his wife Margaret of Denmark (right, with St George). They did not enjoy a harmonious marriage, but both spent considerable time at Stirling Castle.

1371

ROBERT II
becomes the first in a long line of Stewart monarchs. He soon begins repairs at Stirling Castle.

1452

JAMES II
murders William, 8th Earl of Douglas, at the castle during a violent argument.

JAMES V AT STIRLING

Around 1538, James V began his magnificent Palace at Stirling. His months spent in France in 1536, and his marriages, provided James with the wealth, ideas, material culture and skilled European craftsmen. This ensured the creation of a true Grand Design, the like of which had never been seen before in Scotland. The creation of this Palace marked the end of the Middle Ages.

When James V's personal rule began in 1528 he inherited a kingdom almost bankrupted by the regents who had ruled on his behalf. So he was keen to accumulate wealth, and was to marry twice, obtaining handsome dowries on each occasion – a total of £168,750 Scots, a staggering sum at the time. But he needed this money. By far his greatest expenditure was on building, and his second bride, Mary of Guise, was impressed on her arrival by the rich palaces at Falkland, Linlithgow and Stirling.

Above: James V and his second wife Mary of Guise. The Palace was conceived as a Renaissance residence fit for a sophisticated queen from France.

James enjoyed a privileged bargaining position with the Papacy, as a strong Catholic ally at a time when neighbouring England had split from Rome. This brought him powerful friends like Charles V, the Holy Roman Emperor, and Francis I of France, who along with his uncle, Henry VIII of England, showered him with honours.

His European experience had shown him how ideas of kingship were changing. James set out to create a Palace at Stirling for himself and his new queen, incorporating many of these new ideas. They influenced the architecture, decoration and function of the royal apartments, as well as the nature of his court. He wished to be a more distant sovereign, ruling by divine appointment – but he had his work cut out trying to turn his old-fashioned warrior nobles into cultured courtiers. The Palace at Stirling reflects these new ideas of restricted levels of access and greater security, designed to create a heightened mystique around James and Mary while still allowing the monarchs to mingle.

The Palace, together with the existing buildings in the castle, had to serve the needs of new kinds of royal government and court life. Work was at an advanced stage by 1541, with carpenters finishing the stone shell, and it is likely that James took a keen interest in the decoration, including a statue of himself on the outside, and in the subjects of the carved oak roundels for his Inner Hall ceiling.

Mary of Guise bore James two sons, but both died in infancy. James went to war with England in 1542, honouring his duties to France, with only mixed results. But his career turned out to be even shorter than his father's. At the end of the year, he took ill at Falkland Palace and died, leaving the six-day-old Mary Queen of Scots to succeed him.

Above: The Holy Roman Emperor, Charles V, who was also Charles I of Spain. As a hugely powerful Catholic monarch, he was an important ally for James.

Above: Henry VIII, the confident and ambitious king of England. Henry was not so much a friendly uncle to James V as an overbearing neighbour.

1538

JAMES V
begins building his superb Renaissance Palace at Stirling Castle.

1542

MARY OF GUISE
gives birth to Princess Mary, just six days before James's death.

MARY OF GUISE AT STIRLING

James V's marriage to a French noblewoman had strengthened the long-standing political amity between Scotland and France. But on his untimely death, his widow was left in a vulnerable position. She had to act decisively to protect their daughter, the infant Queen Mary. Much of this was played out in Stirling Castle, which belonged to her and was where she sought safety.

The infant Mary was crowned Queen of Scots on 9 September 1543 within the Chapel Royal, where the Honours of Scotland (crown, sceptre and sword) were used together for the first time. The celebrations of this great event may have prompted the completion of the Palace, which would have required the infant queen to take up residence in the King's Inner Hall. From then on, the castle became the main residence of Mary of Guise, until she relocated to Holyroodhouse in the 1550s.

It was here that she held court and fought to protect her daughter's interests. Mary had to withstand pressure from the Earl of Arran,

who had been appointed lord governor, or regent, ruling in the infant queen's stead, and had dynastic ambitions of his own.

Backed by French money and arms, the queen mother built a strong following during the years of instability which followed. Henry VIII pursued a policy of seeking betrothal by warfare of his son Edward to the infant Queen Mary, during the so-called Rough Wooing. Stirling was seen as a safe place for Mary of Guise and her daughter as it was further from the English border than Edinburgh. However, the disastrous defeat at the Battle of Pinkie in 1547 led to the young Mary being sent to France for safety the following year.

Mary of Guise stayed in Scotland and built up her power, becoming regent in 1554, supported by French forces and money. Despite the collapse of so much that she had worked for, she successfully paved the way for Mary Queen of Scots to return from France and rule Scotland in her own right.

Above: The coronation of Mary Queen of Scots at Stirling Castle in September 1543. The ceremony took place in the old Chapel Royal, which no longer stands. Cardinal Beaton, then archbishop of St Andrews, officiated; the crown was held by the Earl of Arran, who at that time was regent. Mary is said to have wailed throughout.

1543

MARY QUEEN OF SCOTS

is crowned at Stirling, barely a year old. After the Battle of Pinkie in 1547, she is sent to live in France.

1554

JAMES HAMILTON, 2ND EARL OF ARRAN

resigns the regency to Mary of Guise, who governs Scotland until her death in 1560.

MARY QUEEN OF SCOTS AT STIRLING

Aged 15, Mary married the heir to the French throne and by 1559 she was Queen of France as well as Scotland. However, the deaths of her young husband and her mother the following year prompted her return to Scotland to commence her personal reign. She returned to a Protestant Scotland at odds with her Catholic faith.

When Queen Mary returned to Scotland, the Chapel Royal at Stirling was the only palace chapel still fitted out for Catholic worship. Even so, at Mary's first service there her illegitimate half-brother James Stewart, together with the Earl of Argyll, physically attacked the officiating clergy, who emerged with 'broken heads and bloody ears'. Mary was distressed by the widespread hatred of the Catholic Church, as communicated to her by the Protestant reformer John Knox, her most implacable opponent.

Mary married her cousin Henry Stewart, Lord Darnley, in July 1565 and the following June she gave birth to Prince Charles James (later James VI and I) in Edinburgh Castle. Two months later, she moved the infant to the secure royal nursery in Stirling Castle. The happiest event for Mary at Stirling Castle was the baptism of her son in December 1566, with full Catholic rite.

The celebrations were largely organised by Mary's future husband, James Hepburn, Earl of Bothwell, whom she had accommodated in the Great Hall. She ordered a bridge built between the hall and her chamber (the King's Inner Hall) to facilitate the baptismal arrangements. A later version of this bridge still joins the two buildings.

Above: Mary Queen of Scots with her first husband, Francis II of France. They became king and queen of France in 1559 but Francis died not long afterwards.

Above: Mary's cousin and second husband, Henry Stewart, Lord Darnley. He fathered her son, the future James VI, but was murdered in February 1567.

Left: Mary's third husband, James Hepburn, Earl of Bothwell. Before their marriage in May 1567, she had granted him quarters at Stirling Castle.

This was the start of three days of elaborate celebrations, climaxing in a full-blown Renaissance triumph, with the mock siege of an enchanted fortress built in front of the castle. Prince James was portrayed as a reconciling hero, besieged by a series of attackers including Moors and 'wild, wykked Hieland-men', all of whom were repulsed. This concluded at night with a pageant of fireworks in the royal livery colours of red and yellow, to proclaim the young prince and the continuation of stable Stewart kingship. This was the first ever firework display in Scotland.

1560

FRANCIS II OF FRANCE dies aged 16, having been king for little over a year. His wife, Mary Queen of Scots, returns to Scotland, where her mother has recently died.

1566

PRINCE JAMES is baptised at Stirling Castle. A year later, he will become King James VI, following Mary's abdication.

JAMES VI AT STIRLING

Top left: George Buchanan, scholar and tutor of James VI.

Above: The imposing entrance to the Chapel Royal, commissioned in 1594 by James VI.

Top right: Mary Queen of Scots depicted with her son, James VI, aged about 17. This is an imaginary composition: the two were separated when he was a year old.

Mary's troubled reign ended with abdication. Again, the successor was an infant, and again there were competing claims for power during his minority. But James VI would emerge as the most enduring and powerful monarch the Stewart line had produced.

Mary was forced to abdicate in July 1567, never to see her son again, and was succeeded by the infant James VI. He was crowned, aged 13 months, in the parish church of Stirling, just outside the castle. Much of James's childhood was spent at the castle, where he was taught in the Prince's Tower (see page 26) by the great scholar George Buchanan. As usual with royal minorities, James became a focus for rival factions.

There were attacks on the castle while the king was in residence in 1571 and 1578, and James was held there as a virtual prisoner after the Ruthven Raid in 1582. During this major insurrection, he was seized by disenchanted Protestant nobles and forced to denounce Esme Stewart, 1st Duke of Lennox, a staunch Catholic whose public conversion to Protestantism had aroused suspicion.

Reports in 1583 on the structural state of the castle suggest that some buildings were close to collapse due to lack of maintenance. One of these was the Chapel Royal, which James replaced with a new building, erected in 1594 in only seven months, to an elegant Classical design. The reason for the haste was so that the new chapel could be used for the baptism of Prince Henry, the first-born son of James and his wife, Anna of Denmark.

Henry's christening was held on 30 August, and marked by a great celebration in the Great Hall, the climax of which was the entrance of a splendid ship which held the fish course, firing volleys from its brass guns, floating on an artificial sea.

Left: An artist's impression of the feast held in the Great Hall at Stirling to celebrate the baptism of James VI's eldest child, Prince Henry.

Below: Anna of Denmark, queen consort of James VI. The Chapel Royal was built for the baptism of their first child, Prince Henry.

1582

ESME STEWART, DUKE OF LENNOX is denounced and banished following James VI's abduction during the Ruthven Raid.

1594

PRINCE HENRY is born at Stirling Castle, the eldest child of James VI and Anna of Denmark. He will die aged 18, without ever becoming king.

A ROYAL PALACE NO MORE

The Stewart dynastic dream to succeed to the English throne was fulfilled by James VI on the death of Elizabeth I in 1603. On moving south he promised many 'homecomings', but he found it surprisingly easy to rule Scotland from England and made only one visit.

Various works were carried out within the castle to make it suitable for the visit of James VI in 1617. It was reported that the west end of the Palace and its galleries had collapsed and 'shote over the craig', so they had to be repaired.

Following the succession of James's son Charles I in 1625, a visit was expected and an even greater programme of works was undertaken. Extensive painting was carried out by Valentine Jenkin, especially in the Great Hall, the Chapel Royal and the Palace, where doorways and fireplaces were marbled. Charles did visit briefly in 1633, during his Scottish coronation visit. Aside from this, the Palace remained empty throughout the 1600s, awaiting a royal visitor.

With such a minimal royal presence, there was little need for major building works at the Scottish palaces, and from this time onwards the military aspect of the castle once again took precedence. Little was done at the time of Charles I's second and last visit to Scotland in 1641, when he was at loggerheads with the Covenanting party in Scotland, and England was on the verge of civil war. Following his execution in 1649, his son was declared king in Scotland, as Charles II, and the English parliamentary army came north on a punitive campaign in 1650. As part of this, General Monck took the castle by siege in 1651, and the scars inflicted by his artillery are still to be seen, especially on the Forework.

Above: A detail from the frieze added to the Chapel Royal in 1628–9 displays the Scottish regalia of Charles I.

Above: James VI in later life. After becoming King James I of England in 1603, he remained king of Scotland, but visited his homeland only once.

After his restoration to the English throne in 1660, Charles II had little inclination to revisit Scotland, but he did agree to rebuild Holyroodhouse as the Scottish royal palace in the 1670s, and extensive work was carried out at Stirling around the same time. He also sent his brother, James, Duke of Albany and York, to Scotland at a time when his open Catholicism was causing offence in England. James visited Stirling Castle on 3–4 February 1681, but despite the recent improvements its buildings were in no fit state for him to stay there.

Above: Charles I, who succeeded his father James VI in 1625. He visited Scotland only twice, in 1633 and 1641.

In 1685, the duke succeeded to the Scottish and English thrones as James VII and II, but he was forced to flee in 1688. He was succeeded by his Protestant daughter Mary and her husband, William of Orange. However, James VII never abdicated, and he and his son and grandsons were to provide a focus of rival loyalty for over a century. Their supporters were known as Jacobites, from the Latin Jacobus, meaning James.

Above: Charles II, son of Charles I. On his father's execution in 1649 he was immediately recognised as king in Scotland, and he based himself at Stirling in 1650–1. He was not restored to the English throne until 1660.

1651

GENERAL GEORGE MONCK
captures the castle on behalf of the English parliamentary army following the Scottish declaration of Charles II as king.

1681

JAMES, DUKE OF ALBANY AND YORK
the future James VII and II visits Stirling Castle, but lodges elsewhere, the palace being unfit for habitation.

THE JACOBITE THREAT

No sooner had a Scottish convention proclaimed William and Mary as joint monarchs in March 1689 than rebellion broke out. Although this was eventually suppressed, it created concern about the weakness of the Scottish castles.

The first Jacobite Rising took place in 1689, under the leadership of John Graham of Claverhouse, Viscount Dundee. Improvements were made to Stirling in response: the two back entrances in the Nether Bailey were closed off, and artillery emplacements were installed on the castle's more vulnerable east side. Naturally enough, such emergency measures paid little respect to the castle's architectural qualities.

If many Scots felt they had no part in the deposition of James VII, they felt even more alienated after Queen Anne came to the throne in 1702, to be succeeded by the descendants of Sophia, Electress of Hanover.

A further incentive to disloyalty was the Union of the Kingdoms. Under James VI, Charles I, Charles II, James VII and William and Mary, Scotland and England were only united by the fact that they had the same monarch. But in 1707 it was decided that the kingdoms should be themselves united, and so the last session of the Scottish parliament was closed on 28 April.

Although James VII had died in 1701, his son, Prince James, known as the 'Old Pretender', continued his family's claim to the throne, and following the Act of Union he persuaded Louis XIV of France to provide a fleet and army to invade Scotland. This fleet appeared off the Fife coast on 23 March 1708 and, despite the fact that the anticipated popular rising did not materialise, it was decided that the principal castles had to be strengthened.

At Stirling the strengthening was carried out between 1708 and 1714, to the designs of Captain Theodore Dury, the military engineer for Scotland. His first proposals, for simply enclosing the area in front of the castle, were criticised and the scheme eventually adopted incorporated parts of the outworks built for Mary of Guise in the 1540s.

The progress of work may have been interrupted by John, 6th Earl of Mar, the governor of the castle and a keen architectural connoisseur, who wished to improve both the royal lodgings and his own accommodation.

However, Mar's involvement at the castle was soon to be curtailed. Following what he regarded as snubs by the new Hanoverian dynasty, in 1715 he instigated a rising on behalf of the deposed Stewart line, raising the standard of the Old Pretender at Braemar on 6 September.

Top left: William II and Mary II, who reigned in both Scotland and England from 1689. Although Mary was descended from the Stewart dynasty, William was of Dutch origin and both were Protestant. Their accession to the throne prompted the first of a string of Jacobite Risings.

Below left: Prince James Francis Edward Stuart, the 'Old Pretender'. As the only surviving son of James VII, he was considered by Jacobites to be the rightful monarch.

Below centre: His son, Prince Charles Edward Stuart, known as 'Bonnie Prince Charlie', who led the last Jacobite Rising of 1745–6. He laid siege to Stirling Castle but was swiftly repelled.

ROBERT BURNS, MRS GRAHAM AND THE STIRLING HEADS

'Here Stewarts once in glory reign'd,
And laws for Scotland's weal ordain'd,
But now unroof'd their palace stands,
Their sceptre fallen to other hands.'

Robert Burns visited Stirling in August 1787 and in this poem deplored the ruinous state of the Palace following the collapse of the ceiling bearing the Stirling Heads. By coincidence, in Edinburgh, Burns had admired the beauty of Jane Ferrier (1767–1846). She went on to marry General Graham, deputy governor of Stirling Castle, and later published her drawings of the Stirling Heads ceiling in a book entitled *Lacunar Strevelinense* in 1817. The Heads had been dispersed but she managed to track them down to make her drawings. This has proved to be an invaluable record, especially since two of the Heads were destroyed in a fire in Dunstaffnage Castle.

Owing to his own inadequacies as a general he was soon in exile in Paris, and while there he found some solace drawing up more elaborate schemes for remodelling the Palace for a restored Stewart dynasty.

The new defences of the castle were tested by the last major Jacobite Rising, in 1745–6, led by Prince Charles Edward Stuart ('Bonnie Prince Charlie') on behalf of his father, the Old Pretender. A few shots were fired as his army marched southwards in 1745, but on his return north in 1746 he laid siege to the castle from the adjacent Gowan Hill. However, the commander of the castle, General Blakeney, made short work of the Jacobites' artillery emplacements when he opened fire from the batteries created on that side of the castle in 1689.

Above: Jane Ferrier, around the time of her encounter with Burns.

Right: Jane Graham's illustration of Stirling Head number 18, which depicts a noblewoman wearing an Italian-style headdress.

1689

JOHN GRAHAM, VISCOUNT DUNDEE leads the first of five Jacobite Risings, each an attempt to restore the Stewart monarchy.

1715

JOHN ERSKINE, 6TH EARL OF MAR abandons plans to reinforce Stirling Castle to launch a further Jacobite Rising.

STIRLING CASTLE IN RECENT TIMES

Despite the rude awakenings of the Jacobite Risings, the castle was becoming a military backwater. There was no reason to carry out more than minimal maintenance of its great buildings: this led to some losses, but also meant that some of its older fabric was left intact.

Long abandoned by royalty, although occasionally serving as a state prison, much of the castle was allowed to fall into disrepair. In 1777, for example, when part of the fine Stirling Heads ceiling of the King's Inner Hall fell in, the rest was simply removed. Such architecture was no longer greatly valued, and there was little money to pay for work which was not militarily necessary. This is regrettable, but one advantage is that minimal change and maintenance resulted in significant long-term preservation.

The situation changed at the end of the century, on the outbreak of war with Revolutionary and Napoleonic France. In 1794 Stirling was the rendezvous when Campbell of Lochnell mustered the Duke of Argyll's Highland regiment. This was one of the two components that eventually formed the Argyll and Sutherland Highlanders, who were based at the castle after they united in 1881. Soon afterwards,

Top: The main entrance to the castle while it was in service as a military base.

Above right: The Palace and Great Hall as illustrated by the architect Robert Billings, who renovated the King's Old Building following a fire in 1855.

there was a drive to provide military accommodation at all the major castles. At Stirling this was achieved by inserting floors and walls in the Great Hall. The hammerbeam roof was removed for the creation of a third floor of barracks around 1800, which also involved replacing windows and adding dormers.

From then on, Stirling became home to varying numbers of soldiers, and the castle's buildings were increasingly adapted to meet their needs. Additionally, several new buildings were raised, from the Main Guard House and Fort Major's House in the Outer Close, to the magazines in the Nether Bailey.

Along with the military requirements, there was growing appreciation of the castle's architectural qualities during the 1800s, and by 1849 it was felt to be worth a visit by Queen Victoria, who thought it 'extremely grand'. It was also admired by Robert Billings, who included views in his influential publication, *The Baronial and Ecclesiastical Antiquities of Scotland*, published between 1845 and 1852. Billings was himself called on to rebuild the damaged parts of the King's Old Building after a fire in 1855, and here – perhaps for the first time – we see an attempt to respect and reflect the castle's historic ambience.

DID YOU KNOW ...

Among the most celebrated prisoners held at Stirling Castle were John Baird and Andrew Hardie, rebel leaders in the so-called Radical War of 1820. Both handloom weavers who had served in the army, they attempted to form a trade union to oppose the introduction of mechanised looms. This escalated to an armed insurrection which was put down at Bonnymuir, near Falkirk, in April 1820. Baird and Hardie were convicted of sedition, and were held at Stirling Castle until their execution at Broad Street in September. On the scaffold, Hardie declared: 'I die a martyr to the cause of truth and justice.' He was cheered by the crowd, which was hastily dispersed by the authorities.

Right: The axe and cloak used by the medical student who acted as 'headsman' at the execution of Baird and Hardie. He was employed to strike off their heads after their death from hanging.

Right: Soldiers of the Argyll and Sutherland Highlanders drilling in the Inner Close.

The army's priority still had to be the accommodation of its soldiers, but there was a shift of emphasis after 1906, when King Edward VII asked that maintenance of the buildings be transferred from the War Office to the Office of Works. This change of responsibility encouraged a more sympathetic climate for the care of the castle's historic structures and, where possible, works were carried out in a way that allowed their inherent qualities to be appreciated.

In 1964, the castle ceased to be the military depot for the Argyll and Sutherland Highlanders. This made further changes possible, though some might have felt that, with the loss of both its royal role and its permanent complement of soldiers, the castle was in danger of forfeiting its purpose. However, in recent years, major works of improvement have allowed what is arguably the finest complex of late-medieval and Renaissance royal buildings in Scotland to be seen and appreciated as the setting for the royal Stewart court at its most brilliant.

1849

QUEEN VICTORIA
visits the castle and deems it 'extremely grand'.

1906

EDWARD VII
transfers responsibility for Stirling Castle from the War Office to the Office of Works, forerunner of Historic Scotland.

ARGYLL'S LODGING

As one of Scotland's principal royal residences, Stirling Castle was a key focus for the royal court, and thus for the great landholding magnates of the nation. Naturally enough, they chose to build prestigious town houses in the streets leading up to the castle. Two of those houses survive today in a remarkable state of preservation.

Argyll's Lodging, the most complete 17th-century aristocratic townhouse in Scotland, was begun in the mid-1500s but not completed until the 1670s. It has been re-created to provide an insight into the luxurious world of Archibald Campbell, 9th Earl of Argyll, and his countess, Anna Mackenzie of Balcarres.

ARGYLL'S LODGING AT A GLANCE

Argyll's Lodging has an air of timeless architectural unity. However, the pink harling conceals a complex building history.

The house was begun in the mid–1500s by John Traill, a wealthy burgess of St Andrews. He constructed a two-storeyed house in the north-east corner of site. Later that century, Adam Erskine expanded the house upwards and outwards, creating an L-shaped tower house. He added two more storeys, a short wing to the south, and a kitchen wing to its west. The courtyard was probably enclosed by this date, containing ancillary buildings.

In 1629 Sir William Alexander purchased this unexceptional tower house and transformed it. He extended the short wing of the tower house southwards, to form an imposing range containing a new suite of principal rooms. At its southern end a further short range returned to the west to balance the main body of the earlier house. This created an elegant C-shaped house constructed around a courtyard and closed off from the street by a screen wall.

The final changes were carried out for Archibald Campbell, 9th Earl of Argyll, in the 1670s. He had the north wing raised by one storey, and the south range extended westwards to meet the screen wall. A further ancillary range, extending southward along the street frontage of Castle Wynd, has since been demolished.

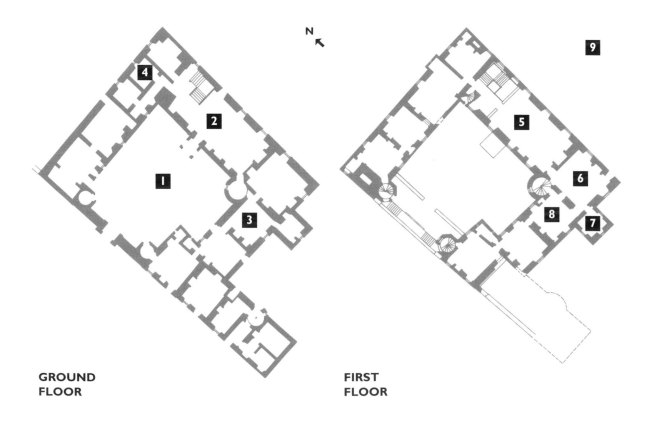

GROUND
FLOOR

FIRST
FLOOR

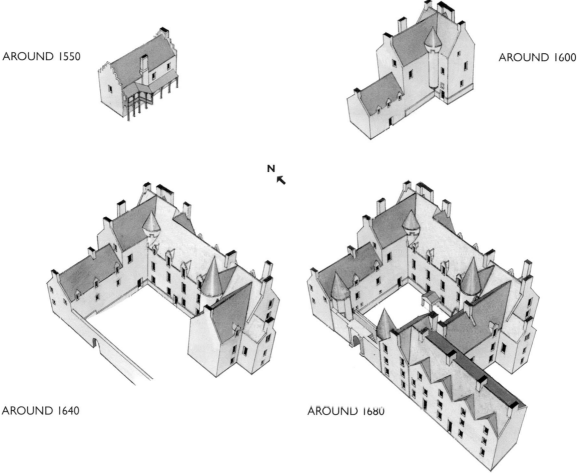

AROUND 1550

AROUND 1600

N

AROUND 1640

AROUND 1680

1 COURTYARD

From here, visitors see the house much as it would have looked in the 1670s. The only major loss has been part of a range along the street frontage.

2 LAIGH HALL

The lower of two reception rooms which were formed in the 1630s. This might have served as a dining room for senior members of the household.

3 SOUTH WING

The ground-floor rooms include an introductory display about the owners of house.

4 ORIGINAL HOUSE

A small kitchen and two vaulted rooms connected by a corridor are the earliest surviving parts of the house begun here by John Traill.

5 HIGH DINING ROOM

The most important reception room in the house. Painted decoration dating to 1675 survives here.

6 DRAWING ROOM

A more private reception room for use by the earl and his most intimate guests.

7 MY LADY'S CLOSET

A small room reserved for Lady Anna's use. Its lavish furnishings are recorded in an inventory of 1680; however, an inventory of 1682 shows significant depletion. The countess may have sold items in these two years to support her husband in exile.

8 MY LORD AND LADY'S BEDCHAMBER

The final and most private room in the state apartment. It may have been used for entertaining guests on occasion.

9 GARDENS

The 9th Earl of Argyll was a keen gardener. The gardens may have been directly accessible from the state apartment.

THE COURTYARD

This tour begins in the courtyard, progressing from the lower-status rooms on the ground floor to a sequence of first-floor rooms which formed the principal apartment of the Earl and Countess of Argyll, before finally returning downstairs and into the gardens.

The courtyard is the best place to observe the architectural finesse and apparent unity of the building. The house developed in four main stages. The work of the first two was entirely subsumed within the expansion of the house, first by Lord Stirling, then by the 9th Earl of Argyll. Externally, the house was lavishly adorned. The corners of Lord Stirling's buildings have buckle-shaped cornerstones, a common motif in the 1630s. The positioning of these on the south façade of the courtyard gives a clear indication of the extent of his house.

The windows were capped with elaborate small gables. At this date only the upper parts of the windows were glazed, with two levels of shutters behind. The present sash-and-case windows were installed by the army during the building's later use as a military hospital.

The Earl of Argyll heightened the north wing, completed the south wing and built or remodelled the range that ran along the street front of Castle Wynd (since demolished). Although the detailing of the earl's additions is more restrained than Lord Stirling's, the decoration of the outer gate in the screen wall is probably his handiwork. The windows and doorways are capped by pediments, some bearing an earl's coronet and the boar's head crest of the Argylls; one doorway pediment is dated 1674.

Above: The north range, whose first-floor windows have pediments bearing the initials of Lord and Lady Stirling.

However, the distinction between the work of the two noblemen is not straightforward. Window pediments on the first floor of the north wing bear the initials of Lord Stirling and his lady – but the pediments on Argyll's south wing are otherwise identical. At the outer end of the north wing there is a doorway at the base of the stair turret with traces of the date 1633. The turret at the outer end of the south wing, dated 1674, is also identical. However, it seems unlikely that the upper floors and stair turret of the north wing in their present form were part of Lord Stirling's work. It seems that Argyll was recording his own contribution along one side of the courtyard and that of his predecessor along the other. Given the close links between the two families, this is not very surprising. It may be seen as recognition by Argyll of the work of his predecessor.

Above: The outer gateway added to the screen wall by the Earl of Argyll in the 1670s.

Top left: The impressive entrance, with a doorway pediment added in 1632 by Lord Stirling. His arms are displayed on the panel above.

Top right: A window at the north-east corner of the courtyard, part of Lord Stirling's development of the house.

THE GROUND FLOOR

The ground floor at Argyll's Lodgings
was mainly used for service accommodation
and by the servants. Its rooms were the
most widely accessible in the house.

THE LAIGH HALL

'Laigh' or 'laich' was the Scots word for 'lower'.
The laigh hall served not only as an entrance
hall but also as the main dining hall for the earl's
senior household servants. There is a splendid
balustraded timber stair at its north end. This
lies within the area of the earlier tower house,
although the present stair is a replacement of
either 1630 or 1675. It was originally separated
from the laigh hall by a screen which does
not survive.

In the 1680s, the laigh hall was simply furnished,
with one long table and fire irons for the elegant
decorated fireplace. A door to the right of the
stairs leads to the gardens. These pleasure grounds
were once extensive but are now considerably
reduced. The 9th Earl of Argyll, like many of his
contemporaries, was a keen gardener and had
several terraces laid out with formal parterres
and walks. Between 1800 and 1964, the army
used the laigh hall as a kitchen to serve patients
and staff in the hospital.

Above: The laigh hall, a less formal reception room on the ground
floor. Members of the household staff may have eaten here.

Inset: The 17th-century staircase leading from the laigh hall
to the main first-floor suite.

'BELOW STAIRS'

The three cellars to the north of the laigh hall lie within the ground floor of the earliest part of the house. At the east end is a small kitchen, with an arched fireplace and a domed bread oven to one side. This was either the 'little kitchen' or the 'baikhouse' mentioned in the 1680 inventories (see page 82). To the west are two further cellars, an ale cellar and a brewhouse. Since both brewing and baking involved yeast the two operations were usually carried out close to each other. Bread and ale were essential elements of the daily household diet.

Beyond these again are the pantry and the great kitchen. In the 1680s, both had tables for preparation, water tubs, a salt basket, pans, stewing dishes, spits for cooking and two great iron grates as well as dozens of plates and trenchers for serving the food. Most of the food prepared in these kitchens would have been supplied from the earl's estates; with much of the county of Argyll as his larder it is unlikely that there would have been many shortages. Smoking and salting were common methods of preserving meat and fish, but it is likely that some food arrived on its own four feet, to be slaughtered and butchered here in Stirling.

Between 1800 and 1964, the army used the ground floor of the north range as hospital stores, although for a time in the 1800s the hospital chaplain had his quarters in the 'great kitchen' and 'pantry'.

Above: The great kitchen on the ground floor of the north range.

FIRST FLOOR: THE HIGH DINING ROOM

The High Dining Room was the principal reception room in the house. It would have been used by the owners to entertain guests at formal dinners.

The High Dining Room is entered via an imposing doorway, its pediment decorated with the earl's initials and a coronet. (However, there is also evidence of the house's later use as a military hospital – the words 'Ward No 1' have been painted above the door.)

In this room the owners would have dined and entertained their guests in fine style. It was sumptuously decorated in the latest fashion. In April 1675, an Edinburgh artist named David McBeath was contracted to paint the room, a task he completed by the following January. His work survives on the wooden partition separating the room from the stair. Elsewhere only small areas of the decoration have survived.

Above: A buxom lady is one of the carvings on the fireplace of the High Dining Room.

Below: The High Dining Room laid out as it might have been for a formal dinner. Afterwards, the tables and chairs could be moved to make way for dancing.

In order to protect the original work while recreating the overall decorative scheme, the design has been copied onto lining paper. It consists of 19 Corinthian pilasters between the dado, or chair-rail, and the ceiling frieze and cornice. The painted frieze sustained decorative unity by reflecting the carved decoration on the fireplace, which dates from Lord Stirling's time.

The panels between the pilasters were designed to display the family's collection of paintings. According to the 1682 inventory, the room held portraits of the 9th Earl of Argyll and his countess, as well as Lady Sophia Lindsay (the countess's daughter by her first marriage) and the Earl of Seafield (the countess's father). Alongside these hung a painting of a ship, a seascape and a still-life of grapes. None of these paintings can now be traced, so the modern reproductions now hanging here include portraits of the 9th Earl, Lady Agnes, wife of the 6th Earl, and the 9th Earl's parents, the Marquis and Marchioness of Argyll. Above the fireplace is *Ships in a Calm Sea* by Van der Veld and to its left *Fruit and Flower Piece* by Verbrugghen. The furniture included 12 folding tables and 30 chairs covered with a yellow stamped material called druggit. These would have been arranged in various combinations for dinner, then moved to the side when not in use or if the guests wished to dance.

Inset left: A cabinet decorated with marquetry in the High Dining Room.

Inset right: The doorway leading into the High Dining Room, decorated with the earl's initials and later labelled 'Ward No 1'.

FIRST FLOOR: OTHER ROOMS

When alone or entertaining honoured guests, the earl and the countess withdrew into their private or state apartments. The first of these was the Drawing Room. My Lady's Closet was entered from the Drawing Room. My Lord and Lady's Bedchamber was the most private room in the house, but even this was used for entertaining.

THE DRAWING ROOM

The Drawing Room was a smaller but altogether more sumptuous room than the High Dining Room. The walls were hung with tapestry, which served as decoration and kept the room warm. The earl sat upon his chair of state with 'twa pein of purpur stamped stuff courtains with an cover for the seat of the same', while his family and guests sat on cane or 'wand chairs' only half of which had 'carpet cushions'.

The room also contained a clock, a finely inlaid cabinet topped with crystal vases for flowers, a fir table, a looking glass and a little carpet – and for entertainment 'ane fyne harp'.

The splendid fireplace is decorated with mythical beasts and the arms of Lord Stirling and his wife. Immediately to its right, behind a wall-hanging, is a doorway (now blocked) that formerly led to a timber gallery overlooking the formal gardens.

Above: A table set for an intimate dinner in the Drawing Room.

Top right: A view of the Drawing Room looking towards the fireplace.

Above right: The chair and cloth of state in the Drawing Room.

MY LADY'S CLOSET

The inventory of 1680 gives us an insight into the personality of Lady Anna Mackenzie, second wife of the 9th Earl of Argyll. This room was where the countess kept her most treasured possessions – several small statues, portraits of her husband and of Mr Baxter, a minister whose preaching she particularly admired, a Cambridge Bible, silver tumblers and gilded cutlery. Also provided were a bell for summoning servants, fire irons and a 'closed stool', or toilet box. Two years later, virtually all that remained were hangings, a chest of drawers, a few chairs and the good Reverend's portrait.

MY LORD AND LADY'S BEDCHAMBER

My Lord and Lady's Bedchamber was used for entertaining only the most privileged guests. The earl may have received his guests while sitting up in bed, a sign of aristocratic condescension. No visitor could have failed to be impressed by the richness of the furnishings, particularly the great bed with its purple stamped curtains and bed cover. There were also matching wall hangings and a closed stool.

There were no corridors within this part of the house: all the rooms interconnected. Behind the hangings in the west wall of the bedchamber is a doorway that once led through to other family rooms (it was blocked up in the 1800s).

OTHER SUITES

The rooms beyond the bedchamber are now inaccessible, but the 1680 inventory gives us some information about their uses. The attic floor of the house contained some family rooms, while the remainder was used as storage (the 'wardrobe') and as a workroom for the tailor. Several other members of the family had suites of two or three rooms each.

Top: My Lady's Closet, the private study of Lady Anna Mackenzie.

Above: My Lord and Lady's Bedchamber, to which privileged guests were occasionally admitted.

THE HISTORY OF ARGYLL'S LODGING

This grand residence takes its name from Archibald Campbell, 9th Earl of Argyll, who bought it in the 1660s and extended it in the 1670s. But its origins can be traced back to the mid-1500s.

We cannot be certain who first built the house. It is likely that it belonged to John Traill, a burgess of St Andrews, who sold it to Adam Erskine, commendator (lay administrator) of Cambuskenneth Abbey, in 1559. Sir William Alexander purchased the property in 1629 and turned an unremarkable tower house into an elegant town house arranged around a courtyard.

The house was completed by Archibald Campbell and remained in the possession of the Campbells until 1764. The building found new life as a military hospital in 1800 and continued in this role for 150 years. Few changes were made to the building during its time as a hospital and later a youth hostel. The building which survives today is still very much a grand Renaissance town house of the late 1600s.

Opposite: A view into the courtyard from the north-west.

Above: The laich hall, seen from the main staircase.

THE FIRST TOWN HOUSE

The main approach to Stirling Castle passed through the market place, in what is now Broad Street. This area and the wynds around it came to be flanked by fine houses of the nobility, alongside those of the wealthier burgesses.

The land-holding magnates of medieval and early-modern Scotland depended on royal favour for their prosperity. They were obliged to undertake considerable duties on behalf of he Crown – including attending the royal court. When the king was in residence at Stirling Castle, some of his principal courtiers were also accommodated there. Others would have had to find lodgings in the burgh. Many of the great families came to see the attraction of building a town house for their own convenience.

The Campbells of Argyll owned various tenements within Stirling from at least the 1300s. By the end of the 1500s, this included the corner plot where Broad Street meets Castle Wynd.

The adjacent property on Castle Wynd was owned by John Traill, a wealthy burgess of St Andrews. In 1559, Traill sold this modest, two-storeyed house to Adam Erskine, commendator of nearby Cambuskenneth Abbey, who expanded it upwards and outwards. Seventy years later, Sir William Alexander acquired it from the Erskine family. Sir William was married to Janet Erskine, and it appears that most of the changes of ownership were between kin or closely related families. Sir William also had close links with the Campbells, who would later come to own the house.

Above: Stirling, around 1680. The castle stands at the top centre, with Argyll's Lodging below to the right and Mar's Wark at the left.

LORD STIRLING'S LODGING

This was a relatively modest residence until 1629, when it was bought by Sir William Alexander (later Lord Stirling). He was the first of two owners who greatly expanded it.

Sir William Alexander was probably born in 1577 at Menstrie, the family seat, held of the earls of Argyll, north-east of Stirling. He was a particularly colourful and favoured character, who was appointed tutor to James VI's elder son Prince Henry, then heir to the throne. In 1603, at the Union of the Crowns, he followed his sovereign to London. He was knighted in 1609 and created Viscount Stirling in 1630.

Sir William spent much of his life dreaming up money-making schemes, most of which failed spectacularly. His most ambitious scheme was the attempted colonisation of Nova Scotia. Alexander sold 6,000-acre parcels of land,

along with the honour of a baronetcy. The scheme eventually lost royal support and collapsed.

The prospect that Charles I (1625–49) would return home to Scotland for his coronation as King of Scots brought with it the hope of a royal presence in his northern kingdom. Alexander decided to improve his new town house in Stirling. When the king arrived in 1633, Alexander was created Earl of Stirling and Viscount Canada.

But despite his rich and varied life, Alexander died insolvent in 1640. The town council soon foreclosed on a mortgage they held on the property. They proposed to turn it into an almshouse but the scheme was abandoned in the 1660s when the Earl of Argyll purchased the property.

Above: Sir William Alexander, who bought the house in 1629 and commissioned major developments.

Above: The armorial panel above the main entrance shows Alexander's arms. He was elevated to the peerage as Viscount Stirling in 1630. On Charles I's visit in 1633 he was made Earl of Stirling and Viscount Canada.

ARGYLL'S LODGING

The final phase of development took place while the house was owned by Archibald Campbell, 9th Earl of Argyll, one of the most powerful men in Scotland in the 1600s.

Argyll was the eldest son of the 8th Earl, who was created Marquis of Argyll in 1641. The marquis is best remembered for his Covenanting sympathies and his conflict with the royalist Marquis of Montrose in the Civil War of the mid-1640s. Although he carried the crown at Charles II's coronation at Scone in 1651, he became a supporter of Cromwell's United Commonwealth of England and Scotland. He paid for this with his life in 1661, following the restoration to the throne of Charles II. The night before his execution, the marquis wrote to his son from his prison cell in Edinburgh Castle, offering him words of comfort and encouragement. Twenty years later, that son, the 9th Earl, would languish in the same prison cell.

Opposite: Archibald Campbell, 9th Earl of Argyll, who acquired the house in the 1660s, and greatly expanded it.

The younger Archibald Campbell was more strongly royalist than his father and, within two years of his father's execution, the family estates and the earldom were restored to him – though not the marquisate. He had married Lady Mary Stewart, daughter of the Earl of Moray, in 1649. They had 13 children, only six of whom survived into adulthood. Lady Mary died in 1668, shortly after giving birth to her 13th child. In 1670, he married his second wife, Anna Mackenzie, widow of the Earl of Balcarres.

The 9th Earl became a firm friend of the Secretary for Scotland, John Maitland, Duke of Lauderdale. The families also became close, Argyll's sister marrying the duke, his son the duke's stepdaughter, and his daughter, Anne, the duke's eldest nephew and heir.

Lauderdale was anxious to raise the royal profile in Scotland. He tried to persuade Charles II to return to Edinburgh and rebuild his palaces. The possibility of court life returning to Stirling may have been the stimulus for Argyll to extend and embellish his residence in the 1670s. But Charles did not return.

Left: The 8th Earl, father of the 9th Earl, officiated at the Scottish coronation of Charles II in 1651, but was later executed for treason.

ARGYLL'S DOWNFALL

Left: A 19th-century painting, *The Last Sleep of Argyll*, depicts the 9th Earl in restful mood on the eve of his execution.

Charles II's overtly Catholic brother, James, Duke of Albany and York, visited Argyll at his Lodging in Stirling in 1681, as High Commissioner to the Scottish Parliament.

James was concerned about Argyll's strong Protestant faith and the scale of his power. That same year the Test Act was passed, demanding recognition of the sovereign's supremacy in spiritual as well as temporal matters. Argyll was among those who would not subscribe to the Act.

Argyll was imprisoned in Edinburgh Castle, tried for treason and condemned to death, but managed to escape to Holland. During his exile, Argyll's Lodging was occupied by his wife Lady Anna. She survived for a while using the income from an estate granted to her by her first husband, the Earl of Balcarres. Charles II eventually granted her a pension, in recognition of Balcarres' loyal support.

In 1685, Charles was succeeded by his brother James, who attempted to restore Catholicism. Argyll was persuaded to lead a rebellion in Scotland, coinciding with an English rising. He struggled to raise an army and was finally captured at Inchinnan, near Renfrew. His earlier death sentence was carried out with little delay.

THE INVENTORIES OF ARGYLL'S LODGINGS

These troubled years are the reason we know so much about the fixtures and fittings of Argyll's Lodging. The 9th Earl's insecurity prompted him to commission inventories in 1680 and 1682, so that he could transfer ownership of the house and its contents to Lady Anna. These inventories provide a wonderful insight into the objects that were deemed of value.

It is clear from the number of beds (17 in all) that there were a considerable number of servants living in the house. Each suite of rooms had additional beds for

servants; some rooms had several box beds with mattresses stuffed with chaff and plain 'stuff' covers, and there is one folding bed.

Privacy in those days was viewed altogether differently. Throughout the house several of the chambers (not just bedchambers) are provided with closed stools, not unlike modern chemical toilets. Such latrines had only become fashionable in the houses of the nobility earlier that century.

A MILITARY HOSPITAL

Top: Argyll's Lodging in use as a military hospital in the 1950s.

Above: The main entrance around the same time.

Argyll's Lodging remained in the Campbells' possession for over a century, but was finally sold on. Eventually it was acquired by the army and put to an entirely new use.

When war with Napoleonic France was declared in 1793, the British Army mobilised on an unprecedented scale. Between 1789 and 1814 the size of the army grew from 40,000 to 225,000 men. The barrack provision was particularly bad at Stirling Castle. The small infirmary in the King's Old Building in the castle was also inadequate. Around 1800, the army bought Argyll's Lodging for use as a military hospital.

The building had several large rooms capable of housing wards, and smaller rooms for use as surgeries, dispensaries, stores and staff accommodation. Fortunately, the army made little impact on the building. Although the windows were altered, most of the original doors and fireplaces still survive.

After Stirling Castle ceased to be a military depot in 1964, Argyll's Lodging became a youth hostel. In 1996 Historic Scotland opened the main rooms to visitors, using replica furnishings to display them as they may have looked when the 9th Earl of Argyll and Lady Anna played out the rather sad days of the early 1680s.

Left: Argyll's Lodging around 1680, when the range running south along Castle Wynd was still standing. The earl and countess are seen arriving at the bottom left.

MAR'S WARK

'On the west of this street the Earl of Mar has a stately house of hewen stone, of curious architecture. The front of it is like to a Port entering to a city, and adds much to the beauty of the town.'

Sir Robert Sibbald, quoted in J. Ronald's
The Earl of Mar's Lodging, 1905

John Erskine (c.1510–72), was the first of his family to become Earl of Mar, and the first to become hereditary keeper of Stirling Castle. He chose one of the most prominent sites in the burgh for an impressive new town house.

GUIDED TOUR

All that remains of the Earl of Mar's quadrangular town house is the façade overlooking Broad Street. This was evidently inspired by James V's palace at Stirling Castle. The embellished frontage, with its fine carving and heraldic panels, was clearly designed to impress. It is clear from the ruins that survive that there were ranges around two other sides of the quadrangle – a layout confirmed by drawings made in the 1700s. Whether the fourth side was ever enclosed is unclear.

THE FAÇADE

The public face of Mar's Wark is wonderfully embellished with nook-shafts and figurative carving, including human and animal masks, dummy gargoyles and statuettes. These sculptures allow us to glimpse the world and ideas of the stonemasons who created them. Prominently positioned above the arched gateway is a heraldic panel containing the royal arms. The heraldic panels on the adjacent towers depict the Earl of Mar's arms. The windows were half-glazed, shuttered and fitted with iron grilles to improve security.

The street frontage was about 35m long. At its centre was an arched gateway, flanked by semi-octagonal towers, and leading via a pend or passage to the courtyard. On the ground floor are nine vaulted basements, most accessible via doors from the street. These provided a secure platform for the main rooms overhead, and were probably used as shops. This was not an unusual arrangement. Across Europe there were town houses of comparable scale which combined commercial and private accommodation in an urban setting.

THE INTERIOR

As only the street frontage survives, much of the internal arrangement of the house is unknown. Two vaulted chambers were accessed through the north tower door. The south door accessed a spiral stair to the upper floors. A reception hall with a canopied fireplace occupied much of the first floor. It was well lit by the windows overlooking Broad Street. The west wall is almost entirely missing. A wall once separated the hall from a smaller room to the north. This room had a fine canopied fireplace in its north wall and may have served as a chamber, or withdrawing room, off the great hall.

Top left: Mar's Wark is now largely ruined, but its Broad Street façade is still impressive.

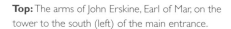

Top: The arms of John Erskine, Earl of Mar, on the tower to the south (left) of the main entrance.

Above: Mar's coat of arms impaled with those of his wife, Annabella Murray, on the tower to the north (right) of the main entrance.

Above: The inscription above the door on the south tower, which reads: 'I PRAY ALL LVIKARIS ON THIS LVGING VITH GENTIL E TO GIF THAIR IVGING' ('I pray all lookers on this lodging with gentle eye to give their judging').

Left: A mysterious figure, apparently a female corpse in a winding sheet, displayed on the north tower.

THE HISTORY OF MAR'S WARK

The story of this building is inseparable from that of the man who built it. John Erskine, Earl of Mar had an eventful and successful career spanning two reigns, and reached the height of his power in the twilight of his days.

John Erskine was a prominent courtier who served as keeper of Edinburgh Castle throughout most of the personal reign of Mary Queen of Scots (1560–7). In 1565, he was rewarded with the earldom of Mar. Two years later, he was removed from Edinburgh Castle by Mary's third husband, the Earl of Bothwell. In compensation, he was granted the hereditary keepership of Stirling Castle, an office which many Erskines had previously held on a non-hereditary basis. This became an important position after Mary's abdication later the same year, for it meant that Mar had custody of the young King James VI.

At the Reformation of 1560, the Erskines had acquired control of the monasteries of Cambuskenneth, Inchmahome and Dryburgh. These lands provided a handsome income to facilitate the earl's building plans. The abandoned monastic buildings also provided the stone from which his new house was constructed. This is confirmed by the existence within the building of several identifiable fragments, including an incised consecration cross.

From September 1571 until his death in Stirling Castle just over a year later, Mar held his most powerful position, as regent of Scotland. He was one of a succession of noblemen who governed the nation during the minority of James VI, and the only one to die tucked up in bed. His predecessor, the Earl of Lennox, was killed during a scuffle in a Stirling street. This event was described by George Buchanan, James VI's tutor, in an account that provides a little information on the progress of Mar's new house:

'[Mar tried to] break through the guarded streets to the market place and at last ordered a body of his musqueteers to occupy his new house, which was nearly finished and overlooked the whole market place, the enemy having neglected to take possession of it, as it was empty and not completed; this afforded a safe station for the King's party.'

Mar's period as regent was dominated by the man who was destined to replace him, James Douglas, Earl of Morton. Morton frustrated every effort made by Mar to achieve peace, and probably hastened his end.

Mar was succeeded by John, 2nd Earl (1562–1634), who grew up with the young King James VI and became his close friend. In 1603, when James became also James I of England, the 2nd Earl followed him to London. By now Mar's Wark was only intermittently occupied.